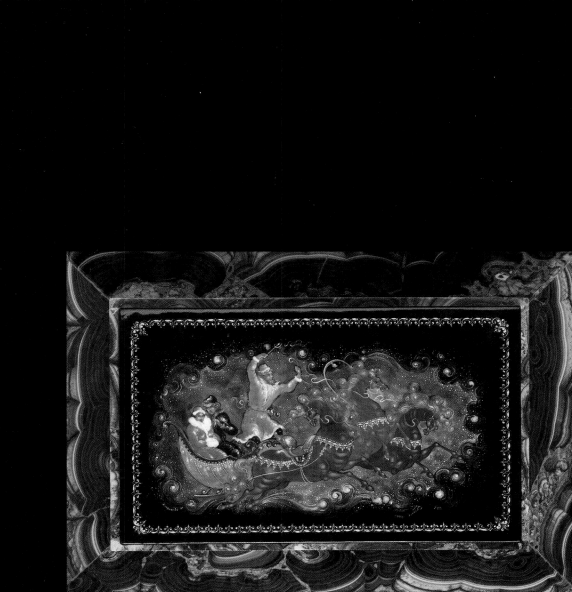

The
iet Union
oday

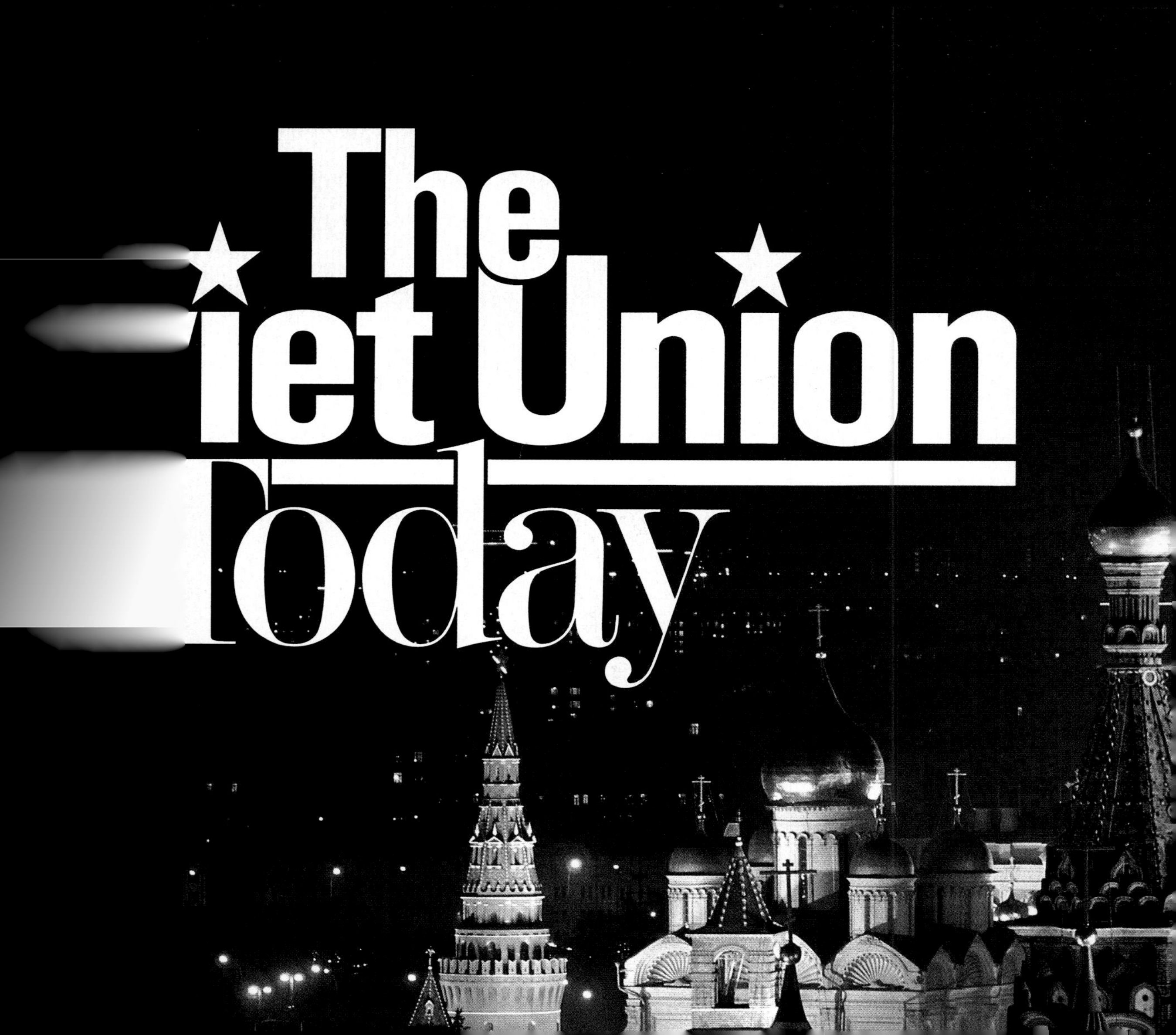

The Soviet Union Today

Published by
The National
Geographic Society

Gilbert M. Grosvenor
President &
Chairman of the Board

Owen R. Anderson
Executive Vice President

Robert L. Breeden
Senior Vice President,
Publications &
Educational Media

Prepared by
National Geographic
Book Service

Charles O. Hyman
Director

Ross S. Bennett
Associate Director

Margaret Sedeen
Managing Editor

Susan C. Eckert
Director of Research

Staff for this book

Margaret Sedeen
Editor

Leah Bendavid-Val
Illustrations Editor

David M. Seager
Art Director

Susan C. Eckert
Chief Researcher

Ratri Banerjee
Gretchen C. Bordelon
Anne E. Ely
Joyce B. Marshall
Melanie Patt-Corner
Kimberly I. Steere
Editorial Researchers

Ratri Banerjee
David F. Robinson
Jean Kaplan Teichroew
Kimberly I. Steere
Picture Caption Writers

Lise Swinson Sajewski
Style

David Ross
Illustrations Researcher

Michael S. Frost
Laurie A. Smith
Illustrations Assistants

Charlotte Golin
Design Assistant

Karen F. Edwards
Traffic Manager

R. Gary Colbert
Executive Assistant

Teresita Cóquia Sison
Editorial Assistant

Jolene M. Blozis
Indexer

Richard S. Wain
Production Manager

Andrea Crosman
Assistant Production
Manager

Emily F. Gwynn
Production Assistant

Manufacturing & Quality
Management
John T. Dunn
Director
David V. Evans
Manager

Carolyn McMartin
Mary Meade Nash
Translators

Robert Hynes
Artwork

Lucy Maxym
Crafts Artwork Consultant

Sergei S. Ivanko
Alexei Pushkov
Oleg Benyukh
Vladimir Zaretsky
Novosti Press Agency

First edition: 165,000 copies
272 pages, 198 illustrations.

Page 1: Palekh lacquer and
malachite box with troika.
From the Lucy Maxym
Collection.
By Steve Adams
Pages 2-3: St. Basil's Cathedral
and the Kremlin, Moscow.
By Nikolai Rachmanov
© 1989 by Desertina Verlag, CH-
7180 Disentis

Contents

Foreword

By Charles O. Hyman

irch trees stand sentinel alongside the highway, their cool white bark in contrast against the forest evergreens.

In memory I am traveling from Moscow to Zagorsk, the famed medieval religious center and monastery 45 miles from the Soviet capital. It is winter. The outside temperature, my driver tells me, is minus 30 degrees. I don't bother to ask if he means Celsius or Fahrenheit. It is so cold it makes little difference. Inside the long black ZIL limousine I am warm and anticipating my visit.

Outside, translucent ice crystals have coated the trees and bushes, which look as if they are made of glass. The color of the sky is the same enamel blue I found on the jeweled eggs made for the Romanov tsars by the House of Fabergé, treasures I have recently seen in the Kremlin Armory museum.

When we arrive at Zagorsk, a funeral is in progress at the 16th-century Church of St. Nikon. Walls of icons reflect the candlelight. A few elderly men and many babushka-crowned women chant devoutly along with the rich-robed priests. The swinging of the censers darkens the already somber scene. Nearby, in a tomb outside, lies Boris Godunov, tsar at the turn of the 17th century. Inside the cathedral next door rests the body of the monastery's founder, St. Sergius, under a silver canopy in a silver sarcophagus—a gift from Ivan the Terrible.

While staring up at these ancient churches, capped by bulbous onion domes, their shape said to echo the helmet design of soldiers from the medieval state, Kievan Rus, I begin for the first time to appreciate the complexities of this vast land. Like so many fortunate people, I grew up reading Pushkin and Chekhov, thrilled to Tchaikovsky's *1812 Overture*, my first taste of classical music, and felt the impact of Sergey Eisenstein's films. But such encounters with Russia's past soon give way when one is confronted by the bustling scenes of cosmopolitan life in today's Leningrad and Moscow, or tries to thread one's way amongst the glistening bodies under the sun on Sochi's Black Sea beach. The diverse peoples of the 15 Soviet Republics speak more than 100 languages. With their long and varied history, they will most likely always be something of a mystery to us in the West, even though we would like the pieces of the puzzle that is the USSR to fit as neatly together as those graduated wooden Matryoshka dolls.

Fascinating results from a recent Gallup survey commissioned by the National Geographic Society showed that one in four Americans could not locate the USSR on a world map and that one in three Soviet participants could not do the same for the United States. Gilbert Grosvenor, President of the Society, has

6

Bark of the *bereza*, beloved birch tree of the Russian countryside.

said that it is "ironic" that "citizens of the two superpowers, whose two nations are most responsible for much of what happens in the world, have so little understanding of it."

Though the international date line separates the United States from the USSR by a full day, few people realize our close proximity to the mainland of that foreign giant which lies a scant 53 miles off the Alaskan coast across the Bering Strait. The Soviet Union is immense. It is the largest country in the world and can comfortably contain within its 40,000-mile boundary all of the United States, Canada, and Mexico. In comparison to our moon, its 8.6 million square miles eclipse the surface area of the near side of that heavenly body. About a quarter of the USSR rests in Europe; the remainder sprawls across Asia. From east to west, its 6,800 miles cross 11 time zones. When night falls upon the western reaches, the dawn of a new day begins in the east.

This nation, historically, has been isolated by geography and climate. It has the longest, and in many ways the most economically useless coastline of any country, blocked by ice on the north for many months of the year. People dwelling in the vast interior region could achieve contact with the outside world only by risking costly and perilous journeys through boundless forests, and across uninhabited icebound lands, arid steppes, and terrible deserts.

Much sooner than the world thought possible there has emerged a new USSR. Now, 73 years after the Russian Revolution, the Soviet Union is attempting afresh to realize its potential. Yet, in a nation that clings so passionately to its memories and reveres its heroes in mighty monuments that would seem appropriate if put up by Texans, there remains a wariness about too much change, too fast. Even as we witness their various attempts at radical reform, citizens of the USSR still endlessly line up to visit Lenin's tomb. We have seen that the changes afforded by *perestroika,* or restructuring, benefit not only the Soviet Union but benefit the West as well. With *glasnost*—openness—access is freer and information flows with a new ease, allowing us a new though still not complete look at this country and its colorful and vigorous people. It has been 13 years since the National Geographic Society published *Journey Across Russia.* Just as we have now, on *The Soviet Union Today,* we worked on the earlier book with the Novosti Press Agency, who then imposed strict and limiting requirements on the author and photographer in exchange for cooperation. Today, however, finding "a mutually satisfactory solution for every difference" was not part of the phrasing of our agreement. In addition, the text and photographs for this book are the work of an international crew, composed of people from the United States, England, France, the Federal Republic of Germany, and the Soviet Union.

When reporting on foreign countries, other publishers by right rarely concentrate on subjects that are of vital interest to the National Geographic. We have set the goals for *The Soviet Union Today* to be the same as those of other, similar volumes we have published: not to emphasize ideology or politics, but to create an intimate portrait that relays a country's past and present, to look at its physical and cultural geography, and to study the diversity of its people.

Across the snow-swept steppe of southern Siberia, a Khakass sheepherder drives his flock homeward at sunset. One of more than 100 ethnic groups in the Soviet Union, the Khakass are typical of Siberia's indigenous peoples—while many pursue their traditional occupations of herding, hunting, or fishing, others have gone to work in the mines and other industries of resource-rich Siberia. About the size of the United States, Siberia is a land of swamp, steppe, taiga, and tundra, with some of the world's greatest rivers and highest mountains. It is the largest region of the world's largest nation.

8

9

Leningrad & the Baltic Republics

By Michael Parfit
Photographs by Jay Dickman

O n the western edge of the Soviet Union, people stand with their backs to the Baltic, between the swamp and the past, between grief and the sea, looking over their shoulders at the future.

The glance ahead is both furtive and unabashed, like the blue-eyed looks young women give young men in the streets of Leningrad at midsummer, when the night streets are filled with silver light and music. In that twilight it is hard to tell evening from dawn, and so it is with the future. The land does not reveal it. From Leningrad, where light itself is geography, to the artificial mountains of oil shale slag in Estonia, to the beloved, poisoned rivers of Latvia and Lithuania, to all the unfenced fields and forests and bogs that hide or memorialize repeated tragedies of disease, hate, and war, the gently rolling landscape of the Baltic region, like its people, appears mild. But like the sea that casts amber on its shores and ties the land together from the Gulf of Finland to Courland Spit, this part of the Soviet Union can be more turbulent than it looks.

"Historically, we are the kind of people who cannot be called open," said Merike Madar, a 38-year-old athlete from Tallinn, the Estonian capital. "We hold all things inside us, in our hearts. But if we have something inside, that will be forever."

I first met Merike in Leningrad, where she was wearing tan greasepaint all over and not much else. It was the first-ever Soviet Union Women's Body Building Championship. Backstage, dark women in tiny bikinis padded through the halls like panthers, practicing in front of mirrors. Onstage a woman danced and flexed to the music of "We Are the World." It was a strange place to think about the hidden determination of a reserved people: the celebration of a sport that even in the West is considered flamboyant. But later, long after Merike had taken her quiet resolve and her many hours of pain out on that stage and walked away with the first-place trophy, it made sense. The quality the peoples of the Baltic have held inside forever, and carry now into the hopeful future, is their determination to oppose the odds of history, to remain obstinately different.

At ten to two on a luminous morning in Leningrad, I began to notice how this edgy game is played. I walked among thousands of people along the Neva River. Peter the Great built Leningrad—then called St. Petersburg—on the Neva estuary between 1703 and 1725, and turned the meanders of swampland into stone-lined canals. One-sixth of the city's 195-square-mile area is water, and the canals and the Neva divide it into 101 islands, which are connected by 620

Detail of woolen mitten knitted in Latvian folk designs.

bridges. Leningrad is charmed by reflections and flow, and its people walk the bridges and embankments as calmly as the water moves, but a quiet restlessness churns beneath the surface.

It was June when I joined the crowds that walked the embankments in informal celebration of the midsummer weeks known as White Nights. It was after midnight but darkness would not come to Leningrad until July. The night glowed with the endless twilight and flickered with the blue lights on top of militia cars. A loudspeaker on one of them boomed. *"Tovarishi!"* it shouted. "Comrades! Comrades! Please excuse the paddy wagon."

The throng along the embankment rumbled with laughter and parted amicably to allow passage for a small blue van. The crowd was awaiting the nightly opening of the Neva River drawbridges to let the freighters in and out of the port of Leningrad. Here at the Palace Bridge were certain rebels who wished to be among the last to cross. The militia was there to stop them.

From the crowd rose the sound of a few voices singing, the faint clash of taped rock and roll, and the aromas of perfume, after-shave, and vodka. Then, from the mass, two young men sprinted up the rising bridge. A tiny police car went after them like a sheepdog, its siren yipping. But the two got away, leaped the widening gap, and dashed into triumphant anonymity on the other side. The crowd cheered. It tolerated the police; it loved the rebels.

Leningrad—a city of more than five million people, the second largest in the USSR—is not politically aligned with the Baltic region. It is emphatically Russian, so does not share the cultural and linguistic animosity to Soviet rule that links the three Baltic Republics. Yet it shares the sea with them, and shares their quiet Nordic nobility.

The people along the embankment were of all kinds: college students; recent high school graduates; black market "businessmen" politely accosting tourists with offers to trade rubles for dollars; workers from the port of Leningrad, where I'd watched wire being shipped to Cuba and aviation oil from the United States coming ashore. One group sang to a guitar, another danced the twist to a tape of "Yellow Shoes," played by a Moscow rock group called Bravo; and under the majestic arch through the headquarters of the General Staff, I passed several boys singing a lament from the Afghan War: "The only friend of mine is a submachine gun." But even the singers were calm and unhurried—northern. They walked the bright night away to the constant and friendly noise that I would become accustomed to during my six weeks in this corner of the USSR: the murmur of voices not raised and the shuffle of shoes on stone.

"People from other cities look at us and understand we are from Leningrad," said Aleksey Voronkov, who was walking down Nevsky Prospekt with his bride of a few hours, Ulya. They were placing flowers on monuments, a traditional wedding ritual. "Leningrad is the revolutionary place," he continued. "It is the heroic city."

Indeed. Earlier I had stood in a small room in the Winter Palace (now part of the magnificent Hermitage Museum) under a music-box chandelier that had once played English folk songs to Russian royalty, looking at the immobile hands of an ornate clock mounted on the back of a rhinoceros. The hands were stopped at 2:10, the moment in the early morning of October 25, 1917, at which Bolshevik revolutionaries burst into the room, arrested the Provisional Government ministers who were meeting there, and changed the course of Russia. Later I walked on shaded avenues among mass graves at Piskarevskoye Cemetery, where behind symbolic stones lie more than half a million people, victims of disease and starvation during the infamous 900 days of the Nazi blockade of Leningrad during World War II.

The memory of that tragedy runs through the heart of the city as steadily as the gray waters of the Neva. Pyotr Sazonov, 83, whom I met fishing from a bridge, spoke of those days as calmly as a farmer discussing a long gone drought. Yes, he recalled it. He had, he said, lost his wife and two children to starvation while he fought at the front, and when he came home he found that his house had been chopped up for firewood. And everyone knows the words of the child Tanya Savicheva, written in her diary in blue pencil:

"Grandmother died on January 25 . . . Uncle Lesha, May 10. . . . At 7:30 a.m., May 13, Mummy died. . . . Everybody is dead. Only Tanya is left."

I spoke to a solemn young poet, Oleg Juryev. In Leningrad, said Juryev, "all this history is life; this is a city in which the dead are not dead."

I remembered what he had said several days later while I was watching young teenagers shoveling dirt and human bones out of an old church in the heart of Estonia. Cheerfully knee-deep in the dust of their ancestors, they were excavating the floor of the 15th-century church in the regional center of Viljandi so it could be turned into a concert hall.

"Most of these people died during the plague about 1730," said the adult supervisor of the work, Jaan Ojasson, a bit apologetically. I wasn't sure if he was sorry about the lack of archaeological attention or that he brought up yet another calamity in Baltic history. He gestured at a large closet stacked five feet deep in the femurs, ribs, and vertebrae the kids had exhumed. "They were not buried properly."

Their rest was still unsettled. Elle Pille, 15, plucked a skull from the closet, held it up like a callow Hamlet, smiled faintly at the infinite jest to which old grief had come, and tossed the skull back into the closet like a basketball.

Thus I came to Estonia, the smallest (17,413 square miles) and northernmost of the three Baltic Republics, and found the people here were also quiet and northern, and immersed in a history of sorrow; but perhaps they were not as solemn as the citizens of Leningrad. Once, it is said, a workman fell from a tower in medieval Tallinn. By chance he landed on a wealthy merchant. The merchant was killed, but the workman survived. The merchant's family demanded that the workman be put to death for murder. The authorities agreed. However, they said, he must be executed by one of the merchant's own family, who must jump off the tower on him.

This glimpse of Estonian justice was offered with a straight face one evening by Peeter Põlluveer, while we stood in the cupola at the top of Tallinn's famous Toomkirik. Peeter was a sturdy, blue-eyed, curly-haired Estonian who spoke excellent English (as well as the Russian all Baltic residents are expected to learn in school) and had been trained as an opera singer. He was assistant to the church's Lutheran pastor. Like many Estonians, he was haunted by the West: His mother watched *Dynasty* on Finnish television; he wrote rock lyrics in English; he watched tourists from Helsinki, just 50 miles away across the Gulf of Finland, pour ashore every day from the ferry *Georg Ots*.

We gazed out over the city, and I saw a marvelous array of ancient tile roofs, spires, old brick walls, towers with names like Tall Hermann and Fat Margaret, shining rails, factory steam, distant apartment buildings like walls of cages, and cranes down by the waterfront. Peeter saw how it must have looked around 1700, when the church and its elevated neighborhood were rebuilt after the great fire of 1684.

"The seashore was much closer," he said, his eyes half closed. "There was a river from Lake Ülemiste. It was a good river. It used to be full of salmon." Swallows flew past the cupola. Peeter's hands flashed in the sunlight like birds themselves. "I look out at Tallinn and I am sad. All these new places, industry, and pollution," he said. "It is best perhaps not to think about it."

W e stood there in silence. I could not help thinking about standing equally high above a gnawed landscape near Kohtla-Järve on the road from Leningrad, in the cab of Novo Kramatorsk Excavator Number One, a 4,000-ton electric shovel that whined inside like a jet, moved as deliberately as an elephant, and took 46-cubic-yard bites out of northern Estonia, clearing overburden off oil shale. Estonia has about 8 billion tons of oil shale reserves, all near Kohtla-Järve, and mines 24 to 30 million tons a year, most of which is burned for heat and electricity. Much of the power is exported to other parts of the Soviet Union.

From the white limestone trench I looked out on old pine forest to the right and new pine forest to the left; the mines have been required to reclaim the land for the past 15 years. But the reclamation doesn't hide the huge piles of waste from the processing of the shale, which loom above the ruins of stone windmills that provided power in past centuries. The people of the area use these new mountains for skiing and hang gliding, and call them "the Caucasus."

Irony was never lost on Peeter Põlluveer. We stood on top of the church looking out toward the peninsula that hid the new Tallinn Port, a modern facility being built by Finnish contractors. At the port I had seen Estonian peat moss—"Superturf"—leaving and Kansas wheat coming in. But to Peeter the port was more than ships and cargo; it was like the strip-mined town of Aiduküla, a symbol of how governments of dominant nations had for centuries been trying to smother the stubborn cultures of the Baltic to make room for their own people. Spasms of Russification under Alexander III and Stalin did not succeed. Recent efforts—major construction works like the port, which some Estonians say was designed to bring Russian workers to the Baltic—have narrowed the Estonian native majority of the country's 1.5 million people to 60 percent.

Although recent concessions by Moscow may give Estonia some economic independence and slow the influx of outside workers, stress remains. One Estonian compared her country to Scotland chafing under English rule; Peeter had a more chilling analogy: It reminded him of Northern Ireland.

We climbed down about midnight. Silver light shone through holes in the roof—the Lutheran Church survives as the dominant religion in Estonia, but it is not wealthy—and Peeter stood for a moment at the edge of the organ loft, looking out into the medieval dusk of the empty church. The Swedish general Pontusson De la Gardie is buried there; so is Admiral Johann von Krusenstern, the first Russian to sail around the world. Peeter was calmed and satisfied by the presence of all this European antiquity. He raised his voice in booming song:

"Swing low, sweet chariot," he sang, "Comin' for to carry me home."

It was always the unexpected, in the Baltic States. One would think, for instance, that the sea itself, which gives its name to the region, would be the central feature of life along its coastline. It is not.

"There is not much of a relationship to the sea here," said Paap Kōlar, standing on the beach at Pirita, near Tallinn, "because no one can get out on it."

Kōlar was a 33-year-old entrepreneur, whose co-op, Hobi, rented windsurfing boards on Pirita Beach. He had fought the authorities for a year—not for permission to operate a marginally capitalistic venture, but to use the Baltic Sea. The sea is the Soviet border and is so jealously guarded that I wondered if swimmers who strayed westward would be harpooned by the coast guard. The beaches were crowded on the hot summer days, but beyond the swimmers in the shallow water and the windsurfers who held close to shore, the sea itself was empty. No sails, no motorboats, no fishermen. The people glanced at it wistfully, as if, like Peeter Pōlluveer, they were remembering a time when it was closer.

They might well have wished for a time when it was cleaner. From the shallow waters off Petrodvorets, the tsarist castle of fountains near Leningrad, where swimmers defied signs warning of dangers to their health, to Estonia's fading resort town of Pärnu, where people bathe in therapeutic mud but are advised not to dip themselves in the Baltic, to the tea-colored Daugava River of Latvia, to the sick rivers and estuaries of Lithuania, the waters were in trouble.

This was no secret. In the new frankness of glasnost and perestroika, it was easier to be self-critical, particularly about pollution. Once, when I asked a party official what he liked about his town, he said, "You may think it is pretty, but we have many problems. Our public toilets are a disgrace."

His town was Palanga, on the Lithuanian coast. At Palanga the ferris wheel turned so sedately it never shut down to let people on and off. At Palanga hundreds of people watched a break-dancing contest with all the intensity of a tennis crowd. At Palanga I watched a man shoot violently down a water slide backwards wearing a tiny leopard-spotted bathing suit and an expression of utter disinterest. A Palanga physician summed it up: "We are a northern people."

In Lithuania, the most southern, the largest (25,174 square miles), and the most rural of the Baltic States, I traveled south from Palanga, and rode a hydrofoil at almost 40 miles an hour from Klaipėda, a strategic port city that has been fought over for centuries. The *Rocketa* dashed past the magnificent long sand dune of Courland Spit and up the Nemunas River to Kaunas, past marshlands and farms, paper mills and cattle, amphibious tanks engaged in military exercises and barges carrying sand.

Like the rest of the Baltic region, Lithuania is a land of glacier-smoothed rolling hills, forests of pine and spruce, broad fields, few fences (dairy cattle are raised indoors from birth to death), and about 2,500 lakes. When you ask people in the capital, Vilnius, what they do on vacation, you hear exactly the same answer you'd get in Minneapolis: "We go to the lake."

Some also go to the river. Along the Nemunas as the hydrofoil shot by, I saw campers and fishermen on the stony banks. But the river was not healthy, and people talked about pollution. Late one night near the tiny town of Zubiskes, 400 people danced into the early morning in a pasture on the bank of the Neris River. It was the first night of a crusade to call public attention to pollution. The next morning the protesters would float down the river by raft. The pasture was full of tents, and early in the evening, leaders of the group held a long press conference in which speakers talked about industry, urban pollution, and tactics. One of several signs staked out in the pasture read: "No more Nemunas, no more us."

Among the signs stood the old Lithuanian national flag, which flew during the brief period of independence the three republics shared between 1919 and 1940. It was three stripes of color: "Yellow for the color of grain," said my guide, "green of the scenery; red blood of the hard past." Not long before, it had been dangerous to show that flag. Now official opposition had eased. "Youngsters wear American flags on their T-shirts," said the secretary of the Presidium of the Lithuanian Supreme Soviet, the republic's number three man. I had talked to him in his marvelous, dimly lit headquarters, which had copper-colored windows and an interior the gold of varnished ash wood and amber. "If people like it, let them do it."

The history of Lithuania is sadly full of people waving flags and dying for it. A few days before the ecological protest, I visited the Ninth Fort in Kaunas, where a monument to the victims of Nazism stood 105 feet high—a flying concrete explosion of fists and faces: "The Unconquered." The Lithuanian guide reminded me this was only the most well-known scourge to cross this landscape. She spoke of two centuries fighting the Teutonic knights' crusade for God and property. She did not speak of Stalin's crusade against national diversity, nor of the years of violent resistance to Soviet rule that wracked the republic after World War II.

"There are many things in the history of Lithuania that we feel pain about," she said. "And this also."

But that night on the pasture beside the Neris, there was only joy. It was like a *gegužine*, the traditional village meeting, informal and friendly, in which neighbor danced with neighbor in the days when almost everyone lived in the country and only the rich people lived in town. Today's young people have moved from the land but remain its children. They fell into the pattern of the *gegužine* without effort. A bonfire was lighted, long-haired young men played the accordion and the fiddle, and people danced the polka and the polonaise on the grass, and when they were tired, sang. "We love these songs," one listener said. "They tell us of the lives of our fathers and grandfathers."

Darkness obscured the banners; the press conference dissolved down the hill. But the bonfire went on and on through the night, the people stood together, and the old songs of father and grandfather and all the dead who are not dead floated out through the pine trees across the river, through the heart of Lithuania, beyond the centuries of grief, toward dawn.

Folk music and dancing themselves carried the banner of nationalism in Latvia, the middle of the three states, a republic slightly smaller but far more industrialized than Lithuania. Latvia has almost 4,000 lakes, but the people's greatest love is for their rivers: the serpentine Gauja that winds for 281 miles through the republic, and the mighty Daugava that begins west of Moscow. The Daugava separates parts of the republic with water but unifies it with affection: "Both sides of the Daugava will never be divided," Latvians sing of their three provinces. "Kurzeme, Vidzeme, Latgalē; they all are ours."

I drove to the capital, Rīga, past unfenced fields and gardens hung with tinsel against the birds. Fields were outlined by natural boundaries of wood and hill rather than ownership; the only straight lines in the landscape I'd seen while flying overhead to Moscow were trenches cut in the peat bogs for drainage. Between fields were forests of tall, slender pine trees, among which wooden fire towers stood 130 feet tall. Latvia is about 41 percent forest. Latvians harvest more than 149 million cubic feet of wood a year, from forests that are mostly young, replanted after the devastations of war and the hurricane of 1967.

In Latvia flowers are almost more valued than trees. On some weekends as many as 400 vendors come to Rīga to sell flowers in the city's huge central market, one of the largest in the Soviet Union. Everywhere in the Baltic States, several collective farms divert labor and energy from the production of food to grow thousands of roses and carnations year-round in huge greenhouses. They are as precious as bread. "Without flowers," asked one Lithuanian, "how would we live?" When there are only 30 to 40 days of clear weather a year, people seem to develop a special hunger for the living reflection of the sun.

For all its flowers, though, Rīga, whose population of about 900,000 makes it the largest city in the three republics, seemed at first to be a weary city. The track and soccer stadium where I ran had once been a magnificent structure. Inside were signs in Latvian and English directing the visitor to the Mechanic, the

Medical Station, the Radio Net, the Hall of Weight, and, at last, to the Room of Rewarding. But while I was there, the entire staff was one unrewarded young man sleeping with his head down on a desktop beside a single fading daisy.

And then there was a parade. It was part of the annual Baltica, a folk festival which moves among the three republics from year to year. It began at the Sports Palace, in an odd melee in which a group of young people bearing a Latvian flag couldn't decide whether to crash the parade. They looked worried; they didn't know the extent of the risk; the flag had not been brandished without reprisals in a major public ceremony since the Soviet takeover in 1940.

Then the doors of the Sports Palace opened, and the beloved Latvian folk group Skandineiki emerged, led by Dainis Stalti, the gray-bearded patriarch of Latvia's folklore renaissance. He strode to the front of the parade. With solemn faces the group played medieval bagpipes and fiddles and a slow drum.

A long ripple of a cheer ran down the parade route, like the sound people made in Leningrad when the boys crossed the opening bridge. At the head of the parade, Dainis carried a huge maroon-and-white Latvian flag.

Behind him in the parade all three national flags—of Latvia, Lithuania, and Estonia—moved down the street like pirate banners, waving defiance. No one arrested the flag bearers. When I had asked Lithuania's presidium secretary about the prohibition of the flag, he had smiled in his ash-and-amber room of power: "That was in the past," he had said. "Many things are in the past. We say goodbye to the past."

The future marched down Lenin Street. The people of Rīga crowded to the sidewalk and balconies, and clapped in time to the drum. The stir ran through Rīga. A northern people was moved.

Dzemma Skulme, one of the Baltics' most famous artists, did not watch. "If I had taken direct part in that parade, I would have been weeping," she told me later, walking restlessly around the floor of her workroom, which was splotched with 30 years of mixed paint. "I sing and dance here." Yet she was an architect of the parade's strongest theme, the survival of diversity.

"Art," she said, "is the best model for pluralism. We now want people to think independently. Art can help." Skulme is not a fringe radical; she is a deputy to the Supreme Soviet of the USSR.

"A year ago," said a member of Skandineiki, "we did not suppose anything like this could occur." Like the defenders of Leningrad, who had survived on "sweet soil"—earth soaked with fat—and grams of bread, these peoples had nourished their uniqueness on scraps for years. Now, unconquered, they were emerging from starvation into a Soviet Union that might learn to value the differences of its peoples.

In the morning after the parade there were reminders of both grief and hope. On Dainis Stalti's window someone had painted that old symbol of hatred, a swastika. But in the square by the cathedral a young couple opened a suitcase and drew a huge line of customers. The pair offered brand new little Latvian national flags for three rubles each, and sold them as fast as flowers.

Gateway to the Soviet Union, Leningrad opens the Palace Bridge on the Neva River to let ships in and out of the port. Twilight bathes the city at 2 a.m. during the white nights of June, when the sun barely dips below the skyline. Tsar Peter I founded the city in 1703, named it St. Petersburg, and made it the focus of his modernization of Russian life.

From a three-room log house on the riverbank the tsar supervised the building of the Peter and Paul Fortress. Its six great bastions stand on an island and were designed to protect Russia from the ever menacing forces of neighboring Sweden.

Inside the fortress walls (between the arms of the bridge) rises the slender golden spire of the cathedral of Saints Peter and Paul, the burial place of this ruler and most of the tsars and tsarinas who followed him—Peter the Great, the original spirit of perestroika.

18

O ctober snow dusts Sunday evening crowds on Nevsky Prospekt in the heart of Leningrad. Bus #10 travels this broad thoroughfare of shops, theaters, and offices along the road that Tsar Peter laid out in 1710 to join the Admiralty—the headquarters of his beloved navy—and the Alexander Nevsky Monastery. Near the Peter and Paul Cathedral, two Leningradkas pause to chat on a bridge, one of 620 spans across the Neva and its canals and tributaries.

In World War II, this now lively, lovely city endured a 900-day Nazi siege. Ruins lay for miles in every direction; 1.5 million residents died. Under blockade, one citizen wrote, "The great streets and squares are dead."

ИРКУТСК
ИРКУТСК
ЙОШКАР-ОЛА
КАЗАНЬ
КАЗАНЬ
КАЗАНЬ
КАЗАНЬ
КАЗАНЬ
КАЛИНИНГРАД
КАЛИНИНГРАД
КАЛИНИНГРАД
КАЛУГА
КАРАГАНДА
КАРШИ
КЕМЕРОВО
КИРОВОГРАД
КИРОВАБАД
КИРОВАБАД
КИРОВСК
КИРОВСК
КИРОВСК
КИРОВСК
КИШИНЕВ
КИШИНЕВ
КИШИНЕВ
КИШИНЕВ
КУЙБЫШЕВ
КУЙБЫШЕВ
КУЙБЫШЕВ
КУЙБЫШЕВ
КУСТАНАЙ
КУТАИСИ
ЛЕНИНАБАД
ЛЕНИНАБАД
ЛЕНИНАБАД
ЛЕНИНАКАН
ЛИЕПАЯ
ЛИПЕЦК
ЛЬВОВ
ЛЬВОВ
МАГАДАН
МАХАЧКАЛА
МИН ВОДЫ
МИН ВОДЫ
МИНСК
МИНСК
МИНСК
МИНСК
МОСКВА
МОСКВА
МОСКВА
МОСКВА
МУРМАНСК
МУРМАНСК
МУРМАНСК
МУРМАНСК
МУРМАНСК
МУРМАНСК
МУРМАНСК
МУРМАНСК
НОРИЛЬСК
НОВОСИБИРСК
ЕЖЕДНЕВНО

Flight schedules fill a wall at the Leningrad office of Aeroflot, the state-owned airline. Travelers queue up at counters under the marble columns and Italian Renaissance splendor of the former St. Petersburg Commercial Bank, built here on Nevsky Prospekt in 1911-12.

Pages 24-25: The embers of imperial Russia glow in Leningrad's Italian and French architecture and ambience—in the golden dome of St. Isaac's Cathedral, the needling spire of the Admiralty, the once grand houses of merchants and nobles along Palace Embankment. Here royal carriages and elite guards promenaded the pink granite walk, and the fashionable society of old Petersburg, late on summer evenings, sailed the Neva in silk-canopied boats rowed by singing oarsmen.

Timm Rautert, Visum

23

S t. Isaac's Cathedral in miniature hardly conveys the scale of the engineering problems met by its French architect, Montferrand, and the half million workers who labored from 1818 to 1858 to erect the massive edifice. Special ships and tackle and a small railway hauled 48 granite pillars, each 114 tons, from a Finnish quarry. Whole forests fell to make foundations in St. Petersburg's marshy ground.

Inside, marble, malachite, lapis lazuli, bronze, mosaics, paintings, sculptures, hundreds of pounds of gold, and a frescoed dome ornament St. Isaac's, designed to rival Europe's greatest cathedrals.

27

Cotton Coulson

P alace Square, developed in the 1800s as a symbol of imperial power, today echoes the tread of a Soviet military band. Here on January 9, 1905, troops fired into throngs of workers petitioning the tsar. Men, women, and children fell by the thousands. Cannon fire boomed in November 1917, when the Bolshevik victory over government soldiers raised the Red flag over the arched military headquarters and the nearby Winter Palace.

Now the palace ensemble, including Catherine II's private retreat, the Hermitage, with its Pavillion Hall (above), forms one of the world's greatest art museums.

G reen groves interlace Vilnius, the capital of Lithuania, southernmost of the Soviet Republics on the Baltic Sea. To the north lie Latvia and Estonia. Over the centuries these republics have lived in subjection to or alliance with nearby nations — Sweden, Poland, Napoleonic France, Germany, tsarist Russia. Following the Russian Revolution, they enjoyed independence from 1919 to 1940, when the Soviet Union took control of the strategic states — avenues to Baltic ports and western Europe.

unk and politics har-
monize in Velyo Vin-
gissar of the Estonian
rock group Vanemode—Elder
Sister. Until glasnost, rock
musicians performed under
tight state control or underground. Now, bearing strong,
poignant, often political messages, they soar to superstar-
dom, record on the state label,

Melodiya, here for sale in
Rīga, and, with official approval, perform abroad.
  Artists too have seen times
change since a 1974 Moscow
exhibit was bulldozed by police.
In Tallinn, a show typifies the
Estonian avant-garde tradition, where abstract individ-
ualism speaks louder than old-
style socialist realism.

Vilnius basketball fans watch the Soviet Olympic team lose an exhibition game to the Atlanta Hawks—105 to 110, in overtime. Win or lose, Soviet fans value sportsmanship. They show respect for opponents and will boo even their own side for rough play.

A waiting contestant limbers up at a 1988 bodybuilding championship in Leningrad, the first in the Soviet Union to include women. Kulturizm, the cultivating of the body, says a Soviet sports magazine, releases tension and sets the spirits soaring.

Pages 36-37: Pollution of the Neris and Nemunas Rivers provokes a demonstration in Lithuania by the Kaunas Ecological Club, part of a growing regional demand for environmental perestroika.

35

Near Vilnius, pasture-land surrounds one of the thousands of glacial lakes that characterize the rolling coastal plain of the Baltic States. Dairy farms, flax fields, and other croplands abound in this region, one of the most productive in the Soviet Union. Slowly, change comes to Soviet agriculture: On a collective farm near Rīga, Latvia, a farmhand forks hay on land leased from the state by the workers, who till it after each day's work for the collective is done.

39

S urf-shop businessman Paap Kõlar keeps an eye on his windsurfing customers out on the Baltic Sea at Pirita, Estonia. Officials may also watch, he thinks, lest someone catch a wave westward and defect.

Sunbathers on a beach in Leningrad share a favorite spot with strollers, bikers, and picnickers. Behind them stands a wall of the Peter and Paul Fortress. Before them flows the Neva River, full of history, legend, and, like the Baltic Sea at Pirita, enough pollution to deter some swimsuit wearers from swimming. Instead they soak up the summer sun with a gusto honed by the long northern winter.

41

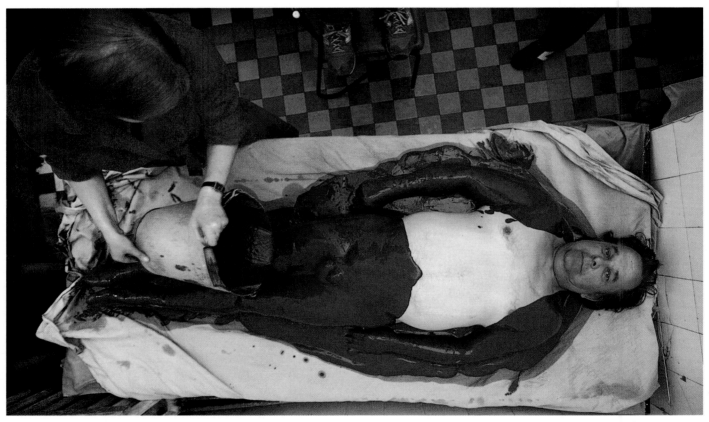

F alling water at an
outdoor pool massages
a guest at the Agricul-
tural Workers' Rest Home in
Palanga, Lithuania. Deft fingers give another guest a fa-
cial. Workers in many callings
earn vacations of two weeks to
a month at such resorts, often
at reduced rates or even free.
    A mud bath clothes a guest
at a spa in Pärnu, Estonia.
The mud, from Baltic Sea
shallows, is said to ease arthri-
tis and other ills; thousands of
patients try it every day.

S lices of amber destined for jewelry gleam under the polishing wheels in a workshop in Palanga. Some 30 to 40 million years ago the amber began as resin oozing from the coniferous forests that blanketed these northern lands. Buried in sediment when ancient seas invaded, the golden droplets hardened into amber, sometimes entombing insects, fruits, leaves, or flower petals.

Today miners dredge or quarry amber nuggets from the seafloor or sedimentary rock. And lucky beachcombers find them washed ashore by storms around the Baltic Sea, one of the world's most important sources of amber.

F lags of Latvia, long suppressed, unfurl anew in Rīga's streets during Baltica, an International Folklore Festival. By day, festival-goers line the streets as a folk group parades in traditional dress. By night, they watch an American group, Kolibri, sing of nationalism and the group's Latvian roots. Of the beleaguered peoples of the Baltic Republics, and their love of music and dance, the Latvian writer Peteris Bankovskis says, "We live, we are, we sing."

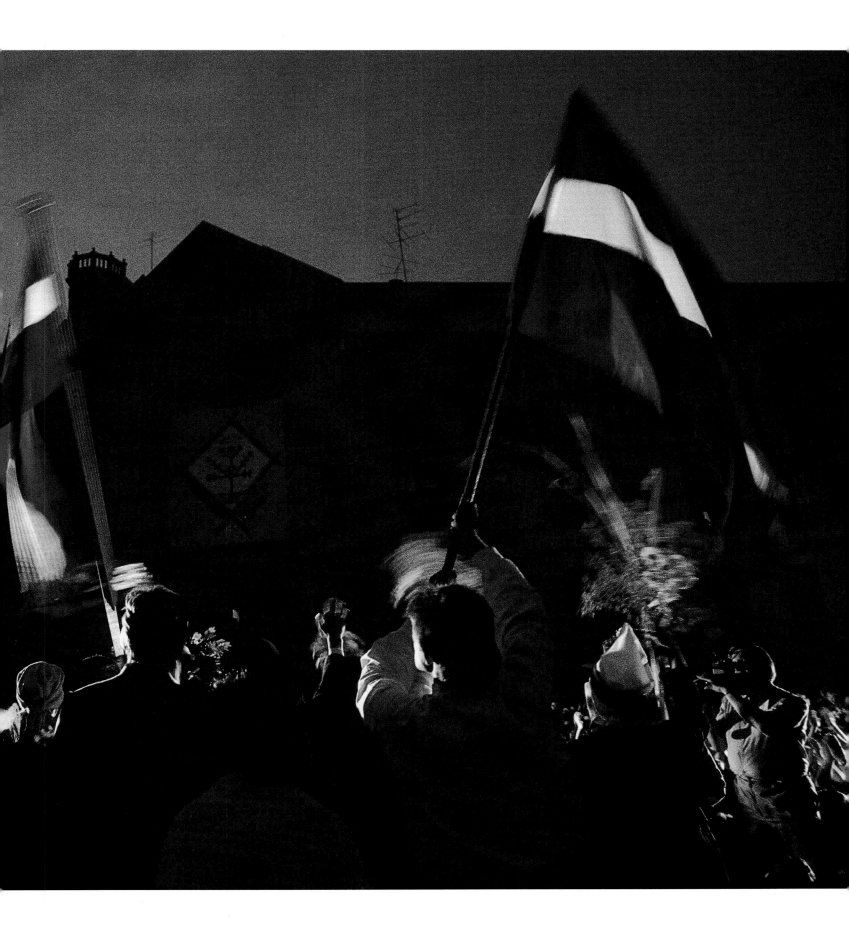

European USSR I

By Lito Tejada-Flores
Photographs by Bruce Dale

even in the morning and the sandy playground of School #74 in the old Novokuznetskaya neighborhood of central Moscow explodes into life. School kids in pressed uniforms holding immense bouquets of flowers chase each other under the shady poplar trees; parents in their best clothes shake hands, chat, fiddle with cameras. Families hurry down the sidewalks of Monetchikovskiy Lane. It's September first, back to school, and no one wants to be late. In the USSR, this moment, a holiday, the Day of Knowledge, has a resonance rarely felt in other countries.

At last everyone is in place: children lined up by age and class in neat rows behind each teacher, boys in blue blazers, girls in white pinafores, red Pioneer neckerchiefs sprinkled like polka dots on the younger classes, shoulder-to-shoulder parents beaming on. The principal at his most dignified, microphone in hand, clears his throat: "Welcome, dear students, to the land of knowledge. School will provide you with the skills and knowledge to become true champions of perestroika and will help you in the struggle to achieve democracy. . . ." It's as down-home as a clambake.

Everyone gets to make a speech: a representative of the parents' association, a retired teacher, a senior student. Finally the director again: "And now the solemn moment has come, the honor of entering school first goes to our tenth graders who are spending their last year with us, and who will also introduce the entering first graders to school." Each senior takes a new pupil by the hand. Two by two they march into the two-story, yellow brick school. Teachers standing by the door are overcome, weighed down with gifts of flowers that every single child has brought. Parents too are overcome, weighed down with memories.

Inside the school the first lesson of the year begins, the *urok mira,* the lesson on peace. In turn students rise beside their wooden desks to talk about Afghanistan, Angola, Central America. Not what I did during summer vacation, but what the world did. The walls are hung with maps.

Russia: a word, a land, a color on the map that always calls up more questions than answers. In the Soviet Union today the visitor is sharply scolded for referring to the country as "Russia," a designation that belongs properly only to part of the Russian Soviet Federative Socialist Republic that sprawls from Europe to the Far East, spanning 11 time zones.

But Russia is also something more than just a place, or a people. Whatever Russia and Russianness may have been, this socialist century has given it a new spin. Today socialist politics is as much a part of daily Russian life as market eco-

48

Motifs from lacquered wooden bowl, in traditional colors used by artists along the Volga River near Gorkiy.

nomics is a part of daily life in the West. Yet there is an essential Russianness that predates the Marxist metamorphosis, a Russianness defined by a vast level landscape and hard northern climate; by a language, religion, and temperament that bespeak an enduring Slavic melancholy; by the brutal punch-counterpunch of historic invasions across the plains and steppe of the Russian heartland.

On the grand chessboard of Russian memories, the Volga River occupies a strategic square. Europe's longest river at 2,290 miles, the Volga always seemed to mark a frontier. Beyond its eastern bank lay Asia, Mongol invaders, and darkness—Batu Kahn's troops in their Golden Horde. And west of the Volga—mother Russia, the Slavic heartland, always threatened, often overrun, saved from barbarian conquerors time and again by Russian princes as barbarous as those they sought to repel. The Volga also has another importance in Russian life. It flows the right way, south toward the sun. Unlike many great Russian rivers that flow north into the Arctic Ocean, the Volga carries its water into warmer regions. And like the Dnepr, also south flowing, the Volga has always worked hard for Russia, still does, as a watery superhighway for Byzantine culture, or for modern freight, ore, and oil; for irrigation; for hydroelectric power.

"Volga, Volga, mat rodnaya—Volga, Volga, mother who bore us," children still chant. This river has seen it all. And today no port along the Volga stirs more memories than Volgograd. Known as Tsaritsyn until 1925, Volgograd today is a long, thin strip of a city stretching almost 50 miles north to south along the west bank of the Volga. It became a Hero City under its next name of Stalingrad—where the decisive and terrible battle of World War II was fought and won, block by block, house by house, where the Nazi advance finally became a retreat. Today it's a great and grimy industrial center, powered since 1962 by a mammoth hydroelectric project just upstream.

Memory is also a major industry in Volgograd. Every summer, white cruise boats of the *Rechflot*, the River Fleet, unload hundreds, thousands of visitors here to climb the monumental, imperial-sized staircases up into town in search of their collective past. Every street, every intersection seems a war memorial of some kind—Red soldiers were executed by White Guards during the Civil War on the city's central plaza, now called the Square of Fallen Heroes. But the grandest temple to the past is *Mamayev Kurgan*, Mamayev Hill.

The hill was the crucial high ground in the worst days of the Battle of Stalingrad. Today boatloads and busloads of Soviet tourists pace off a slow pilgrimage to the summit. Upward through a Chinese-box labyrinth of monuments within monuments: larger-than-life cement statues, pietàs; long ascending walls where Red Army heroes are frozen into bas-relief echoes of their finest hours. A long inscribed line of verse only hints at the cost of defending Stalingrad: "A steel wind whipped into their faces but still they advanced. . . ." A giant hand inside the circular pantheon extends a torch from the psychic center of the Russian earth. The last giant waits atop the hill: a reinforced concrete statue of the motherland, an avenging peasant beauty, 230 feet tall, sword aloft, guarding the high ground, gesturing with outflung arms for her children to follow.

49

By early Friday afternoon, the weekend getaway from Volgograd is in full swing. At a river terminal which looks like a lime green Victorian clapboard stable on top of a big black barge, urban escapees are already waiting for the next ferry to cross the river to the dacha settlements on the low eastern bank. They carry big canvas rucksacks on their backs, string bags full of weekend provisions, fishing poles, and odd scraps of building materials. Once on board, I find myself leaning over the rail near a garrulous old gent with a potato-shaped nose, excited eyes, the mobile expressive face of a circus clown, and a high-pitched voice.

Pyotr Andreievich is a 60-year-old widower, lonely and likable. He once worked abroad he tells me, in Finland building a dam, and he likes foreigners, throws his arm around my shoulder. Where am I going? the first landing on the far side, hell no, come on to the next stop, Kultbasa, another half an hour on the boat, visit his dacha, stay for dinner. *Pochemu nyet?* Why not?

In the Sunbeam dacha colony tiny weekend cottages and large vegetable gardens are randomly tied together by the soft dust of narrow country lanes. Here Pyotr Andreievich built a two-room, two-story dacha 18 years ago, one room over another; here he planted a grape arbor for shade and now ferments red wine in large glass jugs beside his iron bed. Weekend neighbors drop by bringing little gifts, exchanging fish for wine, fruit, gossip. "This is how a bachelor lives in the country," he laughs, taking off his brown suit, putting on shorts and slippers, throwing together a crazy meal—corned beef from a jar, eggs from a neighbor's hen, tomatoes and onions from his garden.

We eat out of the one small frying pan right there on the butane hot plate; then walk a block to the well to draw water in a stainless steel bucket at the end of a 30-foot chain. The mood deepens with dusk: "My father was a Bolshevik, a real one . . . all his life he wanted to join the party but they never let him . . . he tried so many times . . . he was shot in '38, still believing in Stalin. . . ." Back under a bare light bulb, our tumblers of wine are refilled, refilled again. Laughter triumphs in the end. In the end such evenings, that should never end, do. This time with the departure of the last ferry to Volgograd: a 20-kopeck hydrofoil ride back across the starry river. It wasn't the first or last time I would be knocked out by the extraordinary Russian ability to treat people like lifelong friends only minutes after meeting them; or the knack of turning marathon conversations over a kitchen table into unforgettable experiences. *Spasiba.* Thanks.

My Aeroflot jet banks over the sunset surrealism of the Volga Delta in the evening light. Below us are hundreds of gray-green scrub islands, then sand dunes like waves, one after another to a horizon where the Caspian Sea is hiding in the haze. Then long shining leads of water, branching, pencil thin and parallel that I later learn are salt evaporation ponds. Parallel green strips separate the bands of delta water, reflecting like beaten copper in the last sun; the green expands into grasslands with a couple of big river channels coming up to meet us. *Dobro pozhalovat!* Welcome! Astrakhan, southernmost city on the Volga.

Westerners who know about Astrakhan think of *ikra,* salty mouth-watering caviar. The Volga near Astrakhan is one of the great sturgeon fisheries, and this is the season. Close up, the water seems alive, roiling with fish, giant fish, sturgeon thrashing in a slowly shrinking net. The net is being hauled in toward shore by an antique Rube Goldberg power winch, and held, here in the shallows of one branch of the Volga Delta, by a dozen grinning fishermen in oversize yellow waders. Kamil Dzhumaliev, a Kazakh, a big man with sparkling eyes, wades into the middle of this net arena and starts wrestling giant fish into a half-sunken rowboat that serves as a freshwater holding pen. The biggest sturgeon, the pale white beluga, weighs up to 2,500 pounds. Moving them is a tougher job than wrestling alligators, and often it takes two fishermen to hump them out of the net. The sly looking sevruga with their long noses and spotted sides are much smaller. Ordinary garden-variety sturgeon, the osetra, are most numerous and, without being monsters, are still enormous fish, four to six feet long.

This delta scene seems a pastoral parenthesis in a noisy high-speed world. The spiderweb steel cranes and loading docks of a Volga port, the gritty black tankers full of Baku oil, are a million miles away. Cool southern sunshine glints off splashing water, writhing fish. The shouting, joking roughnecks of the 20th Party Congress Fishing Collective wait while their net is hauled back out into midstream. The vacationing family of Leningraders camped out under Russian olives 50 yards away dive off the bank and splash in the mud. Pampas grasses and tall reeds bend and dip in a gentle breeze. Hauling the net out and slowly winching it back in is a cyclical 45-minute process, so there's plenty of time for cigarette breaks and talk while most of the guys wait on shore. An American writer is such an oddity in these parts that I'm deluged with questions. Politics? Not interested. The hot topic is the cost and performance of American cars.

Back in town I run headlong into hipness, Russian style. Hundreds of Astrakhan teenagers are enjoying the last balmy evenings at the open-air Youth Disco, just inside the white walls of the old kremlin. This is the full-on, bop-till-you-drop boogie: kids in stone-washed jeans, strobe lights stuttering, filtered spots on the walls of an old tsarist ammunition storehouse flicking their red, blue, and green light over the moving crowd, 16-year-old deejays on stage with their poised patter and banks of reel-to-reel recorders.

The music is very international, very loud, very good. This summer's hits blast from stacks of speakers at 9-on-the-knob: Status Quo's "You're in the Army Now"; a sultry French ballad, *"Voyage, Voyage"*; a German number that begins: "Ladies and Gentlemen, the President of the United States" followed by synthesized Reaganspeak and the sound of nuclear blasts. The kids cheer every song. Not long ago rock was a decadent Western vice and those who loved it were labeled hooligans; today rock is a canonized Soviet art form; tonight it's a tribal rite without frontiers. I meet Nautilus Pompilius, a Russian group famous for surrealist lyrics and songs about Stalinist crimes. Above the dancers a yellow moon lights up old walls, battlements, spectral towers. This is where the rebel Stenka Razin pushed tsarist officers out of tower windows to their death on the cobblestones in the 17th century. Tonight the courtyard is a solid mass of jiving youngsters. They all sing along: *"Mini, mini, mini—minimum sideniya. Maxi, maxi, maxi—maximum dvizheniya!* Minimum of sitting. Maximum of movement!".

From Volgograd, instead of heading southeast to Astrakhan and the delta, one can slow the pace and float west along the Volga-Don Canal into the old stronghold of the once feared Don Cossacks, a population of savage fighters made up mostly of Tatars and runaway serfs from Great Russia. By linking the Volga with the Black Sea, the Volga-Don Canal was designed to dramatically expand river freight throughout the western USSR. The 60-mile-long canal was finished in 1952 and touted as a major engineering marvel. Thanks to the canal, almost every town along the Volga or Don refers to itself today as a "port of five seas" (the Black, the Caspian, the Baltic, the White, and the Sea of Azov).

Surmounting the first and last locks are enormous triumphal arches out of a Stalinist fantasy. And the whole canal with its 13 locks is decorated with extravagant statuary, monumental wedding cake towers, rusting metal haut-reliefs and gold-painted lampposts—a genuine if slightly tarnished imperial facade. Barges full of black iron ore glide through in slow motion.

Past the canal, one follows the River Don almost to the sea before landing at *Rostov na Donu,* a beautiful city that wasn't totally destroyed in the Great Patriotic War. Downtown Rostov is still full of low, old-fashioned, two-story 19th-century buildings: pale plastered walls, dusty yellows, beiges, and pinks, with peeling casement windows. And full of energy.

This city of a million souls is a hotbed of the new cooperative movement—one of the more intriguing options in Mikhail Gorbachev's perestroika. In Rostov too, I learned how a few months earlier 20,000 local petitioners had defeated a plan for a highly polluting municipal trash incinerator. The campaign had been led by a university physics professor, Yuri Dumbrovsky, waged in the council chambers of the local soviet, in the letters to the editor columns of local newspapers, in town squares and parks. A campaign that ended in permanent municipal funding for the Rostov Ecological Committee, and seemed to be a confirmation of the view that conservation is a task for citizen-activists.

The trip back to Moscow by train is a classic iron-horse cross section of Great Russia, south to north, 22 hours on the *Tikhii Don,* the express that bears the name of Sholokhov's famous Cossack novel, *And Quiet Flows the Don.* As we pull out of the Rostov on Don station, passengers are pulling on pajamas, housecoats, sweat suits, slippers. The woman who doubles as concierge-conductor in each car brings us glasses of tea along with sheets, pillows, and blankets. It's going to be a long ride.

Our first stop in fading afternoon light is Novocherkassk, the 19th-century Cossack center. Grapevines hang from a pedestrian overpass above the tracks; pigeons and sparrows practice peaceful coexistence on the warm asphalt platform, pecking at sunflower seeds and crumbs; small loudspeakers in the train corridors are playing soft, innocuous Euro-rock rhythms. The station seems full of evening quiet, yesterday. It's an old world, the old world.

Oak forests line the track, spotted with a few yellow leaves, a half-moon rises in the east. The forest is only a thin screen beside the tracks, and through breaks I can see newly harvested fields, some freshly plowed, some still covered with stubble. 8:00 p.m. At Zverevo, a sleepy country station, the last light disappears. A few old-timers are talking in front of the ceramic-tiled station, the platform benches are all broken, and everything looks dingy except for the treasured flowers in large cement pots. We enter night like a long tunnel.

Morning, rolling north—small villages emerge from shadow, streets are mud and puddles, rows of white geese parade single file. Sometime during the night we've crossed an unmarked border into autumn. This morning the hedgerows are yellow-brown, the trees yellow-green, the sky dull gray. On station platforms, waiting for local trains, I spot the first fur hats, *shapkas.* Women stand muffled in giant blue overcoats with knitted wool beanies pulled mushroom-like over their ears. At grade crossings the twin sisters of these women emerge from tiny brick cabins to raise their tightly rolled yellow signal flags. Here and there, in vegetable gardens rushing south past the windows, a few giant cabbages are still lying on the ground, bigger than soccer balls, bigger than beach balls.

Overnight everything seems to have changed except the land itself: wide flat spaces and more wide flat spaces; occasional rolling hills; fields stretching to half-hidden horizons. This tabletop landscape runs all across the Russian Republic and its neighboring republics, east too into Asia, without a single mountain range to block the fast-moving Arctic air masses that sweep all the way south to the Caspian in winter, freezing even the Volga at Astrakhan for three months. Hour after hour, the wintry fields and fringes of autumnal forest flicker by the train. Nineteenth-century travelers would have seen essentially this same stretched-out panorama, this wide landscape that stubbornly resists change.

Moscow, however, is as modern as things get in this part of the world. The Soviet capital is a fast-paced urban pressure cooker, a landscape of opportunity: bright lights, big city, *Moskva,* where an awful lot of Russians would rather be, even though some young people sport buttons that read *"Khochu vuh Pareesh—* I'd rather be in Paris." Twelve million people pack the capital on any given day: almost nine million official residents; two million daily visitors and unknown thousands of illegal residents who take their chances without a *propiska.* Obtaining this official permit to live in an attractive metropolis like Moscow is sort of like getting a green card to work in the United States, only harder. *Vremenyi,* temporary workers, come to Moscow for the same reasons people everywhere migrate to big cities, more jobs, more action; they're looking for the future.

But the capital is also a place where you can slip seamlessly back into the past. Some of Moscow's subtlest memories are made of stone and plaster: the perfect art nouveau buildings on Kropotinskaya Street. The painted plaster of 19th-century mansions, deep ocher, pistachio green, and blue with white plaster trim—and only those little black glass plaques, State Committee for this or that, to remind you what year it really is. Moscow is full of old neighborhoods: some famous, others that you only discover after hours of aimless walking—narrow streets hidden behind the massive facades of big avenues.

Moscow is a city you can get sentimental about. You sit on a wrought iron bench along Sretensky Street, cool sunlight filtering through linden and maple leaves. Next to you, tangled in each other's arms, a young couple hides under an overcoat because they have nowhere else to go; Alla Pugachova's sad ballad, "Ferryboat Man," plays softly on their transistor radio. You watch preschoolers run crazily across the fallen leaves while grandmothers scold and gossip. The neighborhood is so old and out of the way that there aren't even any lines in front of the stores. And you think, *my God, what a beautiful place.*

Or a city to get furious at when you realize that city planners have widened perfectly good streets into ugly 12-lane boulevards that act as wind tunnels in winter. Or built the barest, starkest new suburbs you've ever seen. Or created a traffic pattern where left turns at intersections are virtually impossible. The Muscovite solution to this last problem is ingenious and restores a little faith. A dozen little Zhigulis, Zaporozhets, and Moskvichs pulling off a synchronized mass U-turn in the middle of a block, like a school of fish suddenly changing direction, is a pure form of urban ballet.

Moscow memories, Moscow names: Mayakovskaya, Pushkinskaya—a glance at the Moscow subway map tells you that Russians would just as soon name squares, streets, and metro stations after poets as politicians. It's a good sign. An afternoon walk on the Arbat is even better. The Arbat is a new and very successful Moscow experiment: a refurbished historic district turned into a long pedestrian zone. The Arbat is full of strolling young people, jugglers, painters, street musicians of all kinds, classical violinists to Dixieland combos . . . and poets! In Western countries such pedestrian malls are old news. But where else in the world can you see a crowd of 250 listeners immediately collect around a young poet as soon as he starts to perform?

Where else are poets and poetry this important? Vladimir Vysotsky is still the best loved poet-balladeer a decade after his death in 1980. His antiestablishment songs, during the Brezhnev years, circulated across the whole country in home-dubbed cassettes. One evening on TV I saw a film clip of Vysotsky singing his ballad, *"Ya Nye Lyublyu—* I Don't Like"; and thereafter, every time I repeated those three words to a Soviet acquaintance, the lines of the song would come tumbling out, as if from a national memory bank:

> . . . *I don't like cold cynicism . . .*
> *or people reading my letters*
> *looking over my shoulder. . . .*
> *I don't like myself when I'm afraid. . . .*

Vysotsky's poetry is strong and direct, his recorded voice gravelly and intense. But I find the love his ballads inspire even more remarkable than the poetry. His grave under the birch trees in the old Vagankovskoye Cemetery is perhaps the most visited shrine in the Soviet Union after Lenin's Mausoleum, revered for different reasons, in a different way. In front of a complex bronze statue of the poet, where an upside-down bronze guitar strapped to his back turns into a halo, where wild horses of bronze burst from his shoulders and metamorphose into wings, visitors have left a red, white, yellow, and magenta sea of asters, gladiolus, chrysanthamums, daisies, a ritual of remembrance.

A few steps away different memories animate a different ritual; the Church of the Resurrection is packed, overflowing. By the door, a tall bushy-bearded priest showers holy water out over the densely packed crowd pushing up the steps, a press of babushkas, old women in bright paisley or flowered or plain scarves. Although it's midday not midnight, autumn not April, this small ocher-plastered church regularly celebrates the service usually reserved for Easter. The Krestniy Khod, the procession around the church, has just finished, tall skinny tapers clutched in old hands. Inside, the Resurrection responses echo like shivers. *"Kristos voskres"* drones the priest. *"Voistinu voskres"* chant the old women who make up 90 percent of the congregation. ("Christ is risen." . . . "Truly he is risen.") Candles are passed forward from hand to hand to be lighted and placed in gilt stands beneath the icon wall. In a side chapel a funeral is proceeding in parallel with the main service. In open coffins lie the dead, three very old women in very black dresses. White headbands of paper printed with Old Church Slavonic characters circle the dry parchment of their pale foreheads.

Now it's way past midnight and a low ceiling of mist off the Moskva River sparkles above empty streets. I'm walking back to my hotel after a grand night of Armenian brandy and kitchen-table talk, exhausted and stimulated by what must surely be the Russian national sport, the epic supercharged all-night conversation that knows no frontiers, no limits, no rules. In a store window on lower Gorky Street, a giant blood red face, half skeleton, half mask, grins me to a halt. It's a poster soliciting contributions for a memorial to the victims of Stalin. A couple of tiny automobiles, moonlighting as taxicabs, whine across the empty square in front of the Manège, the old imperial riding school, the big downtown hotels are dark geometric silhouettes. In Red Square the cobblestones are wet from mist, the red glass stars on the Kremlin spires glow weakly through the filter of fog.

Without warning the clock on the Spassky Gate strikes 3:00 a.m. Like shots, explosive footsteps wake me from my Moscow musings. It's only the changing of the honor guard before Lenin's Mausoleum: hourly on the hour. Two soldiers and their commander, goose-stepping in slow motion, rifles balanced on the palms of outstretched hands. The tomb is lit but the red granite no longer looks red, the row of blue spruce trees under the Kremlin wall hides in shadow. Shadows, echoes, and memories own this immense empty space. The thousands of tourists have left no traces. Across the square, from behind the GUM department store, the first street-cleaning ladies—stooped old women with twig brooms—are arriving on silent slippered feet. Another day. In another world.

Windows of the huge, modern Hotel Rossiya frame the faceted, many-colored domes of the oldest building in Red Square, the 16th-century Cathedral of St. Basil the Blessed. The name of Moscow's great square, Krasnaya, *carries a double meaning: In Old Russian it was "beautiful square." Modern Russian "red" shares the same root word. Now Russians see their historic square as both red and beautiful.*

Moscow began in the 12th century as a small post on the Moscow River, to secure control of water routes from the Baltic Sea to the Caspian. In 1918 it became the capital of the Soviet state. Moscow's status as the capital of Russian Orthodoxy, first recognized in 1322, was reconfirmed in 1988, with the celebration of the millennium of Christianity in Russia and a relaxation of state opposition to religion.

57

itizens shop Moscow-style at GUM, the first state-owned department store. Gosudarstveniy Universalniy Magazin (State Universal Store) is an immense three-storied, glass-covered arcade completed in 1893 under Tsar Alexander III, and taken over by the Soviet government after the revolution. Despite chronic long lines and short supplies, GUM attracts some 250,000 shoppers a day. In contrast, the spirit of free enterprise operates in parks and streets where vendors sell anything from paintings to pets to jewelry.

A skim of December ice covers the Moscow River as it flows southeast through the city. Above the embankment rise the "Stalinist gothic" towers of one of Moscow's largest residential buildings, 30 stories, with some 700 apartments. One of seven prominent buildings erected during the Cold War era of the 1940s and 1950s, its design fulfilled the government mandate to "create outstanding works of socialist architecture which reflect the glory and greatness of the Stalinist epoch." Such buildings today are usually the cherished homes of elite citizens.

61

Vladimir Vyatkin

Vladimir Vyatkin

Music and joie de vivre draw Muscovites outdoors. A guitarist performs on the Arbat, a pedestrian promenade that supports a counterculture of musicians, artists, and poets. In front of the Bolshoi Theater, a nostalgic audience listens to a World War II veteran play his accordion. To celebrate Soviet Army and Navy Day, February 23, the Moscow Winter Swimming and Training Club prepares to plunge into the icy waters of the Moscow River. Hardy groups like this are known as Walrus Clubs for their eagerness to brave winter chills.

F lowers for the teacher and the traditional lesson on peace highlight first-day ceremonies at Moscow's School #74. Most of these children will join communist youth groups—the Little Octobrists, Young Pioneers, and Komsomol. In kindergarten, youngsters sing, "We are Lenin's Grandchildren!"

Pages 66-67: An ornate flag-pole base on the roof of the Grand Kremlin Palace overlooks the Kremlin and Moscow past and present. An ensemble of cathedrals, royal residences, and administrative buildings, the Kremlin testifies to eight centuries of religious and political power. Today, although many of these architectural legacies of church and state have been converted to museums, the business of government still takes place within the Kremlin walls.

65

B| iblical scenes and stories from Russian history cover the walls and ceilings of the Hall of Facets, the tsars' largest audience room in the Kremlin. Mikhail and Raisa Gorbachev received the Reagans here at the 1988 Moscow summit.

Carl Fabergé, jeweler to the Russian court, created many of the Kremlin's treasures. This jeweled Easter egg celebrates 300 years of Romanov rule. Resting on a gold pedestal portraying the imperial double-headed eagle, the egg displays diamond-encased portraits of notable Romanovs, from the first, Mikhail, tsar in 1613, to the last, Nicholas II, assassinated in 1918.

E very hour, at the peal of the clock in the Kremlin's Spassky Tower, the guard changes at the Lenin Mausoleum. Winter and summer, processions of citizens and tourists file endlessly across Red Square and into the tomb to view in somber quiet the embalmed body of Vladimir Ilich Lenin, the founder of the Soviet state.

On Lenin's desk in the Kremlin lie memorabilia from 1918 to 1922, the years during which the revered leader lived in the Kremlin and, in this office, received peasant and diplomat alike.

70

O n a bank of the Volga, 530 miles southeast of Moscow, mountain climbers scale the "Motherland," on Mamayev Hill in Volgograd, to give the 230-foot-high concrete monument its annual touch-up of water repellent. Mamayev Hill, solemn with its massive statuary, memorializes the loss of thousands upon thousands of Soviet lives during the bitter 1942-43 Nazi siege of the strategic Volga city.

73

The still waters reflecting houses in Minsk belie the turbulent history of the capital of the Byelorussian Republic. A focus of trade since the 11th century, Minsk has been scarred and devastated by wars, invasions, and fires. Yet, in keeping with its name, which comes from menyat *(to change)*, Minsk has always rebuilt on its ruins. Following the massive destruction of World War II, the city rose again, to become an industrial and cultural center.

76

A red army awaits shipping orders at the Minsk Motorcycle Factory. The women spraying paint on fenders and inspecting gas tanks belong to a work force of 6,500 employees who turn out 227,000 motorcycles and 860,000 bicycles a year. Long waits for scarce and expensive cars have made these alternative vehicles popular. Minsk, with its many factories, is one of the fastest growing cities in the USSR and accounts for a third of the industrial production of the Byelorussian Republic.

he Golden Key #17, a school that cares for children aged 2 to 6, is one of nine schools sponsored by the Belaz Truck Factory near Minsk. Day care is just one of the many benefits arranged for the approximately 11,000 employees and their families. Soviet factories often construct housing and subsidize rent and food with extra payments or factory stores for their workers, who also enjoy recreational facilities such as auditoriums, swimming pools, and stadiums. Labor turnover is low and sometimes three generations of a family work, sleep, and play under the auspices of the same plant.

One way to get to know a town is to visit the market. Here in Kazan an open-air market becomes a center of life as citizens meet and gossip, buy and sell. Small private plots such as Kazan's suburban gardens provide the Soviet people with more than half of the total potato crop each year, and almost a third of other vegetables, as well as significant quantities of fruit and flowers, pigs and chickens. The produce raised by private entrepreneurs demands premium prices and is considered to be of higher quality than that sold in state markets.

81

Work and home for members of the Red Star Fishing Cooperative lie downriver from Astrakhan on the Volga Delta, one of the world's prime sources of sturgeon caviar. Strict rules governing the season and the areas where fish can be caught are part of an effort to increase sturgeon populations depleted by many years of river pollution and diversion by dams. Sturgeon fishing for the Red Star is limited to peak spawning times in spring and summer—seasons when fishermen for generations have set out their nets by nature's clock.

European USSR II

By Paul Shott
Photographs by Bruno Barbey

cross the steppe that covers almost half of Ukraine, the green train sped south toward Kiev. Not a bend in the track, nor a curve as far as I could see. I reflected with pleasure that I was on the road again, exploring parts of the Soviet Union I hadn't seen in years—Ukraine, where my family is from, and Moldavia—the southern region of the Soviet Union that has so often found its fortunes linked with events in the rest of Europe. I was anxious to see how life there had changed and how it remained the same.

Through the window of my compartment I watched the evening sun dip in the direction of the Carpathian Mountains. Southeast of the Carpathians, between the Prut River and the Dnestr, and on the southwest border of the USSR, adjoining Romania, is Moldavia, after Armenia the smallest of the Soviet Republics (13,012 square miles). Moldavians, who are ethnic Romanians, make up two-thirds of the population of four million, along with Russians, Ukrainians, Czechs, Bulgarians, and others. With its fertile soils and friendly climate, Moldavia grows fruits, nuts, vegetables, and grains, and concentrates much of its industry on wine making, sugar refining, and other processing of the generous yield of its land.

The Carpathians arc for some 150 miles across western Ukraine. In the south the Crimean Mountains rise sharply along the Black Sea coast. Otherwise, it is the steppe that rules Ukraine, sometimes rolling, sometimes cut by river valleys and ravines. It is now highly cultivated but in places one still sees what Anton Chekhov saw at the end of the 19th century—grasslands and "a boundless plain," where low "hills melted together into rising ground, which stretched right to the very horizon and disappeared into the lilac distance."

In population, Ukraine is the second largest of the republics, with more than 50 million people; in area, its 233,000 square miles make it third, after the Russian Republic and Kazakhstan. Or, to measure by a scale perhaps more compelling in today's climate of ferment, if Ukraine were an independent nation, it would be the second largest in Europe and potentially one of the richest, with agricultural as well as industrial wealth.

Kiev, the capital, claims more than 60 nationalities from Eastern Europe and the USSR. When our train pulled into the city in the early morning coolness, the waiting rooms and platforms presented a cultural collage typical of the region. Central Asians with handlebar mustaches and black-and-white embroidered skullcaps carried melons and potatoes in *avoskas*, the string bags named for the reason they are usually tucked into pockets: "just in case" one finds some-

84

Embroidery from the Carpathian Mountains, Ukraine.

thing to buy; although in this case, the produce might have been carried north to sell first. Two almond-eyed women, their long black hair braided, wore bright head scarves and lots of gold jewelry. They talked quietly, as is characteristic of Soviet culture, and never smiled. There was a group of soldiers, so young they must have been inductees, all short, husky, with dark skin and jet black hair—I guessed Uzbeks or Kazakhs, or maybe Siberia. They wore black boots, and their tunics, casually open at the neck, were draped over tight trousers and held by the regulation heavy brown belt with brass buckle and embossed Soviet star. In the 20 minutes it took to load our van, I spotted people of at least a dozen nationalities. In Kiev, I met engineering students who were Gagauz (a Turkic stock), Gypsy singers, a Lithuanian nurse, a Bulgarian dancer—and my old friends Lucy and Pyotr. She is Russian, he is Polish, and both are English teachers.

The September sun was hot when Lucy, Pyotr, and I carried a picnic lunch to an island in the Dnepr, the great river that flows through the city and empties into the Black Sea. As we enjoyed our meat dumplings, pickled beets and mushrooms, and black bread and butter, I looked westward toward the steep riverbank where 1,400 years ago the Slavic prince Kiy fortified a settlement that would become the rich and powerful state of Kievan Rus. What I saw was history stitched to topography: the river that carried traders and invaders; the hills of Kiev with the imposing bronze figure of Prince Vladimir who adopted Christianity in 988 and, according to the old chronicles, urged it upon his subjects by dunking them in the Dnepr; the panoply of golden onion domes of the Pecherskaya Lavra, the Monastery of the Caves, the cradle of Russian Orthodox monasticism. Amidst the thick green trees that make Kiev so beautiful, clusters of old buildings stood out like islands; bright white walls encircled blue and white churches whose glittering domes pierced the crown of treetops.

On another sweltering afternoon we strolled along Taras Shevchenko Boulevard, named for the beloved Ukrainian poet, and Kreshchatyk, Kiev's main street, so glorious with its shops, wide thoroughfares, flower beds, linden and chestnut trees, that people compare it to Fifth Avenue and the Champs Élysées. Sidewalk vendors served long queues of people waiting for ice cream, pastries, candy, and Pepsi-Cola.

I joined the line for kvass, a thin, dark brown brew that tastes like root beer without the fizz. It is dispensed from tank trucks on the street in every city. For 15 kopecks the kvass seller, dressed in a long white coat and high white hat, hands you a glassful; you stand to one side and drink it down, then return the glass, which she rinses with water and fills for the next customer. Today stores sell kvass concentrate, but I remember my grandmother making it from scratch. She steeped rye bran in water, in the bathtub, added boiling water, let the mixture ferment, then strained it.

Pyotr told me that when the Russian Orthodox Church celebrated its millennium in June 1988, religious leaders from around the world filled the city. For the first time, Soviet television showed church services nationwide. Crowds gathered on Shevchenko Boulevard where loudspeakers broadcast the choir of

St. Vladimir's Cathedral singing, "Sacred Rus, safeguard the Orthodox faith, for in it is your affirmation!"

St. Vladimir's is one of 22 operating houses of worship in Kiev, and when I went there it was packed. To move from icon to icon or from one side altar to another required patience and many repetitions of *prostite, pozhaluysta*—excuse me, please. Six priests officiated at the three-hour service. Thick incense curled to the ceiling. From the back of the congregation, people handed forward thin yellow candles to be lighted and placed in holders at the front. Men and women knelt and touched their heads to the floor before altars, icons, tombs, or at the feet of a priest. When I left the cathedral, I paused by the door to drop five-ruble notes into containers marked "restoration," "maintenance" (donations pay priests and staff), and "bread"—for the poor.

When I flew to Donetsk a few days later I encountered the stuff that Lenin called the bread of industry—coal. Near the end of the flight I saw dark brown hills rising sharply in the distance—strange, I thought, on this flat steppe. As the plane banked through a metallic gray smog, I could see scores of the cone-shaped peaks towering over the 20-story apartment buildings nearby.

In Donetsk there are over a hundred of these *terrikonniki,* smoldering heaps of tailings from the 22 coal mines under the city. The top of one, I thought, would give me a great view, so early one morning I chose a hill from my hotel window and began to hike toward it through a poplar grove and across a grassy field spotted with daisies. There were no buildings, no vehicles or machines, no people, only silence and, soon, an acrid stench of sulfur dioxide that brought tears to my eyes and stung my nose and throat. I knew that I should not be here! At the base of my hill a few small bushes poked through the rubble, and rain had furrowed large gullies in its sides. I began to climb but stumbled in the loose rock. Every step brought more rock tumbling down on me as I fell repeatedly. Then, sliding, I lost my camera. I gave up. Later, still fascinated, I asked permission to try again. *Nyet.* It is forbidden to climb the "explosive" *terrikonniki. Nyet.*

But there is more to Donetsk—over a million people and at least as many green shrubs and rose bushes. The city has a song: "One Million Roses." On Artem Street in front of a cinema an old woman in black was clipping a garden that formed the face of a clock. I spoke to her, using the Russian *roza,* but she did not understand. Then she smiled and, with the Ukrainian word *troyanda,* handed me a yellow rose.

More gardens decorated the grounds at the Zasyadko Combine when I went to explore one of its three coal mines. An engineer, Andrei Grigoryevich, greeted me in the courtyard, where miners sat on benches among the roses, reading, smoking, talking, playing chess. After a briefing in the office—the mines employ 9,000 workers, extract 5,600 tons of coal every day, pay an average wage of 480 rubles a month, have 94 miles of tunnels—Andrei and I headed for a long, red brick building. In a side room, next to a large area with showers, a steam room, and a swimming pool, we began the half hour of outfitting with which every miner starts his shift. I hung my street clothes on a hook and stood naked. A woman in the ubiquitous white work coat and hat handed me my gear.

Andrei showed me how to put on miners' "socks": Place each foot in the middle of a large strip of white cloth, fold the cloth over, bring it up to the ankle, and tuck in the end. Next came a cotton garment that resembled the two-piece long johns I wear in the New England winters. Then, black wool trousers and shirt, a brown belt, and knee-high black rubber boots. I clipped a miner's lamp onto a blue metal helmet, strapped a battery to my right side, hung a gauze mask around my neck, and slung a foot-long oxygen tank over my shoulder.

A rattling, bouncing cage of an elevator, operated by two women, carried us half a mile underground, where we headed for a tunnel, turned on our helmet lamps, and trudged for an hour and a half over log-strewn tracks, jumping puddles of sooty black ooze, in a space so cramped that I hit my head on the roof scores of times. It was cool and breezy from the fresh air pumped into the shafts, but soon I began to sweat and pant. All around me the men were bare chested, black from waist to hairline. At the face of the coal seam they worked kneeling or on their backs, scooting and slithering around log and concrete roof supports. Not one wore a breathing mask. There was silence, broken only by the sounds of work or by an occasional "Come here, I need you." They were repairing the coal cutter—a 30-foot-long machine with a cleated wheel—that advances along the face shearing slabs and chunks of coal onto a conveyor belt.

In the miners' canteen there is a poster on the wall: "Quality with perestroika." In the hallway a banner read, "Perestroika is everyone's duty," and another, "There is no turning back."

I sat in the canteen sipping tea with Fyodor Borisovich, a 37-year veteran of the mines and a brigade leader firmly in favor of the new work laws governing the combine. Now wages are based on production, efficiency, and quality—not, as formerly, on quotas set by Moscow. But, said Fyodor, "last week one brigade received 25 rubles, another 14, and another only 9." Everyone laughed as he asked, " What would your wife say if you came home with 9 rubles?"

I knew that I had seen a *pokazukha* mine—one that, although real enough, is "for show" to foreign visitors, and I was sad because I knew that life for many miners is much harder than anything I had witnessed. The summer of 1989 focused the world's attention on Soviet coal mines, when strikes spread across the nation. Donetsk miners expressed bitter grievances that had built for years. Among a long list of demands, they asked for better mine safety, higher wages for night shifts, longer vacations, dependable supplies of food and other consumer goods, improved housing, an end to corruption among mine officials, and—what may turn out to be most important in the long term—trade unions independent of Moscow and the Communist Party.

During my stay in Donetsk I saw much evidence of the industrial power of the Donets River basin, or Donbass, as this part of the USSR is called. Here in eastern Ukraine the land doesn't present the expansive, pastoral sprawl to the horizon as it does in so much of the central and western portions. The plains become hilly, cut by deep, wide ravines and gullies. The terrain is broken up by great windbreaks of poplar, ash, and elm to protect crops from the *sukhovey*— hot, dry air accompanied by strong winds. Donbass coal and the iron ore and steel mills of nearby Krivoy Rog were the early foundation of Russian industry and are still vital resources. In between, at Nikopol, on the Dnepr, lies the world's largest manganese deposit.

One day we drove north toward Kharkov. Like most major highways in Ukraine, the road went straight through cities. In Konstantinovka, an industrial center of some 100,000 people, a chemical plant stretched for miles. We passed a factory that makes windows for motor vehicles, and another that produces loco-motives. In Slavyansk, a chemical center, there were long, white factory build-ings, tall smokestacks, a monorail carrying buckets of soda from open-pit mines, and, mirroring Donetsk's *terrikonniki,* huge, white hills of soda debris.

At the Donetsk Lenin Machine Construction Factory—it employs 7,000 people who manufacture 60 types of equipment for the coal industry—I was guided by a plant administrator, a trim man with a mellow voice and an athlete's physique. Not exactly my idea of a bureaucrat. As we stood in the din of the fac-tory, beneath a new yellow coal loader with tires taller than we were, I ques-tioned him about perestroika. He looked me squarely in the eye. "This plant paid 80 percent of our profits to the government last year," he replied. "In the future we want to keep 60 percent." He expects approval for that as well as per-mission to sell products to the West. He pulled me closer and cupped his hand to my ear so I could hear him. "First we must improve our quality."

There's a lot more color to life in the Soviet Union than most outsid-ers suspect. The city of Odessa, a 200-year-old port where the steppe meets the Black Sea, showed me a montage of beauty and ro-mance: cobblestone streets; balconied, baroque buildings in a pal-ette of glowing pastels; catalpas, acacias, lindens, and chestnut trees; the rose-gray granite Potemkin Stairs that sweep down to the sea. I spent much of my time in Odessa strolling with a map of the 19th-century city in hand. The old street names tell of Odessa's melting pot heritage: French Street, Greek Street, Jewish, Moldavian, Spanish, Polish. Now they're all renamed. On Push-kinskaya (formerly Italian) Street, the ornate concert hall is evidence of another proud Odessa heritage. Among the famous musicians who came from Odessa are Jascha Heifetz, David and Igor Oistrakh, Emil Gilels, and Sviatoslav Richter.

At a pedestrian mall, I watched a photographer take pictures of children posing with a small monkey. There were folk singers and artists and a line where 60 people stood waiting to buy *Modern Cuban Detective Stories* for three rubles a copy. I went to a nightclub where the show included a magician, acrobats, a dog act, six dancing girls who wore purple feather boas, pasties, and little else, and a break dancer who twisted, humped, spun on his stomach, leaped from the stage to the dance floor, and ended by backflipping onto the stage. He'd learned it all, he told me, from American videos.

On one of Odessa's sandy beaches I met Lydia, a svelte 27-year-old into *kulturizm*—bodybuilding. She was the first diet conscious person I'd seen in the USSR, although there is a growing movement. Lydia and her husband, Andrei, a professional long-distance cyclist, followed a plain diet without the pickled foods, pastries, and tea that most Russians are so fond of. They had come to Odessa to watch competitions in swimming, cycling, and running, and were two people who might be called *zabolelshchiki*, slang for "sports fans" but literally "people who have a disease" or "people who are sick."

I had seen plenty of those in Kiev—thousands of people in a drenching downpour in the Central Stadium cheering for the Kiev Dynamo, their beloved soccer team. Beloved because Soviets are crazy about sports that may win them Olympic medals, and beloved because they cherish the memory of the martyred Dynamo players under World War II occupation who beat a German team, knowing that they would be killed if the Germans lost. I sat in the rain with the plastic-draped crowd, listening to their shouts, whistles, hurrahs, and a rhythmic "Sasha, Sasha, Sasha" as a favorite midfielder slid across the wet grass.

There was a brass band in the soccer stadium and, the next day, a brass band at the Kiev Hippodrome, where fans wager on thoroughbreds, sulky and troika races, and polo games. With a screaming crowd, I watched troikas from Ukraine, Kazakhstan, and the Russian Republic compete for a silver trophy. For another race I decided to place a bet myself, and lined up at one of ten windows, where a female attendant—a *bukmaker*—insisted that I had to pick two horses to win in order, something like our perfecta. For two rubles I chose #3, Flicka, and #2, Fantastic—and they did it! I saw nothing posted about odds but I was happy to exchange my small, brown, unreadable paper stub for five rubles.

I left Odessa, headed for Moldavia, riding in the back of a green van. Up front were the driver, Georgi, and his wife, Marie, both Ukrainians. With the luggage they had packed two blue 15-liter cans—not for extra gasoline but to bring back homemade wine they would buy from the country people.

The two-lane highway, a main route between the Soviet Union and Eastern Europe, was crowded with trucks spewing black exhaust, tourist buses, big blue-and-white tractor trailers labeled SOVINTERAVTO (a Soviet export company), and passenger cars—small Ladas, black-and-white Volgas. Many of the cars bore plates from Romania, Czechoslovakia, Hungary, and Poland, and strapped on top of every one were boxes and bags, gasoline cans, tenting gear, baby carriages, and other goods the travelers had purchased to take home.

There was no idle land here. After we entered Moldavia, every square foot seemed to be plowed and planted—an agronomist told me the figure is 85 percent. Even village streets contribute. One I saw was lined with pear trees, another with pomegranate. Now it was harvesttime. Convoys of trucks poured down dirt roads onto the highway, carrying loads of onions and tomatoes to canneries in Tiraspol or Bendery. Men, women, and youngsters on work brigades sat along the roadside, awaiting transportation to and from the fields. Horse-drawn wagons laden with walnuts, sugar beets, and eggplants pulled into depots where their produce would be graded and loaded into big, open green trucks.

In some ways my stay in Moldavia was like being in an old-style Soviet movie full of propaganda about the rich earth and happy peasants, but this was real. Near Soroki, a town on the steep right bank of the Dnestr, we drove through a 4,500-acre apple farm. In every direction, row after endless row of trees undulated across the low, rolling hills. To make sure that the apples were picked before cold weather, the usual labor force of 1,000 was enlarged to 2,500. Many of the workers were students on their "labor semester," a regular September assignment. Near a barn, 14 girls sorted lower grade apples destined for stewing or juice. As they worked, they sang Moldavian songs about love and marriage.

I picked grapes the following day with a brigade of students from an agricultural college. At lunchtime a sort of Moldavian chuck wagon appeared—a large, open truck, behind which everyone immediately lined up. Standing on the truck bed, a heavy, talkative woman unlatched the lid of an enormous kettle of steaming cabbage-beet-and-chicken soup. In quick order, she grabbed a bowl from a wooden crate, ladled it full, took two or three slices of black bread from another box, plopped a big gob of soft butter on the bread, and put the meal in an outstretched hand.

When I had received my lunch I picked up a spoon from a box on the running board and joined a group of seven young women. We ate sitting on the ground or perched on upended pails. I got a lesson in how to juggle soup bowl, spoon, and bread, and another in how to tie headkerchiefs, which they all wore low on the forehead with the triangle tied at the back, not under the chin as Ukrainian women do. One of the women, Dorina, used me as a model for the scarf-tying, an exercise that commanded the attention of the entire brigade. When I stuck my Dallas Cowboys cap on top of the properly tied scarf, everyone screamed with laughter and then all the men insisted on a turn wearing the cap.

Conversation there, as with young people I spoke to in Yalta, often revolved around the desire to see something of the world outside their own country. Oleg, a tall, long-haired, green-eyed, 19-year-old Yalta native, seemed to make a career of cultivating foreign tourists and vicariously soaking up Americanism. In exchange, he offered me a revealing, if casual, glimpse of a way of life quite different from that of the young Moldavians.

Yalta can be reached only by land or sea (or an occasional helicopter). This vacation and health resort on the tip of the Crimea, a peninsula reaching into the Black Sea, has no piece of land large and flat enough for an airport. Many of the millions of yearly visitors approach, as I did, from Simferopol, the capital of the Crimea. The road to Yalta at first follows the valley of the Salgir River, a stream that flows from the Crimean Mountains. It is the arc of these three parallel ranges rising at the edge of the steppe that blocks north winds, shielding Yalta and several smaller towns that cling to the mountainsides along the narrow stretch of rocky seacoast.

Our car climbed past orchards and vineyards and twisted through a narrow gorge to reach the pass across the mountains. From there the road dives in sweeping curves, the forested mountains close on both sides. Suddenly the sea comes at you, with Mount Medved (Russian for "bear") crouching at the edge, and there is Yalta, its buildings—from Tsar Nicholas II's Italian Renaissance palace, now a sanatorium and museum, to tiny houses—etched against the cliffs.

The next day brought a warm October sun, a beneficent season called babushka—grandmother—time. The summer crowds were gone. I bought three yellow roses from a white-bearded Tatar, who wrapped them in newspaper and cautioned me to carry them with the stems pointing upward and the blossoms toward the ground—no special reason, he told me, except that this is the proper way. I found slot machines—this was new!—in the Hotel Oreanda, and another surprise. It is now owned by a British firm, a mark of new economic policies.

Above the city the jagged summit of Mount Ai-Petri overlooked green, thickly forested terraces. I walked along Franklin D. Roosevelt Street (named in commemoration of the 1945 Yalta Conference of Churchill, Stalin, and Roosevelt) and found the same restaurants, the same bookstores, almost nothing changed from the Yalta that I remembered.

The weather had turned cool when I met Oleg at an outdoor café. Oleg likes black—black T-shirt stenciled "Finland," black Italian jeans, black Reeboks. "My greatest dream," he said, "is to own a black Porsche." He was incredulous when I told him that I don't own a car and don't really want one. Oleg's mother is dead and he lives with his grandmother. He has no job. Asthma, he said, prevents him from holding a good position. I got the idea that this suited him just fine.

We strolled along the Lenin Embankment, lined with palm trees. The sea was black. Waves pounded the retaining wall and sprayed the pavement. Children played a game with each incoming splash, running up to the wall and then back just in time to avoid a shower. Like brilliant balloons, Portugese men-of-war by the hundreds rode the water.

With Oleg I sat at a table near the embankment's edge. Oleg and his friends went about fully clothed—they didn't bother with suntans—while, below us, autumn's tenacious bathers from colder regions sunned against the wall. To Oleg, Yalta is a boring place. "Too many old people. Nothing to do." I wasn't surprised to hear that he would like to live in Moscow.

Oleg can buy marijuana any time he wants—local officials claim that ships coming into Yalta are the source for drugs, although, nationwide, the government is acknowledging more and more a serious problem—and for amusement he and his friends walk up and down, night and day, along the embankment. The brave ones talk to foreigners, who will get them into the hotels and nightclubs reserved for tourists.

I protest—"But you have the mountains and the sea."

Oleg spread his arms wide. "What is in between for me?"

This made me sad. For me there was so much between the mountains and the sea.

At harvesttime near Kishinev, the capital of the Moldavian Republic, pensioners help out, sorting corn for a few dollars a day and a basketful of farm produce. From corn, women prepare mamalyga, a cornmeal porridge that is a national dish of Moldavia.

Tiny Moldavia and its giant neighbor, Ukraine, are called breadbasket, granary, garden of the nation. With their relatively mild climate and rich black earth—chernozem—they produce about half of the Soviet Union's fruit, sugar beets, and sunflower seed, and a quarter of its grain and vegetables.

92

A village in southwestern Ukraine—with its houses typically strung along a road and close to water—lies in territory that has been Turkish, Polish, Austrian, and Russian. Yet its people are mostly Ukrainian—Slavs like Poles and Russians, but with a distinct culture. Ukraine, briefly independent after the Russian Revolution, and Moldavia both have long been disputed among European powers. The Moldavians are ethnic Romanians; in 1939 part of Moldavia, then under the Romanian flag, was handed to the Soviet Union by a pact between Hitler and Stalin, carving up central Europe. The agreement changed the boundaries of Ukraine, giving it land from eastern Poland and from the Soviet Moldavian Republic—and giving the USSR political advantage as well as industrial and natural wealth.

Here the Russian soul was born, in Kiev, the mother of Russian cities. October Revolution Square, with its fountains and tall buildings, honors modern history, but it stands along Kreshchatyk, a street which long ago was a wooded valley, a hunting preserve of the princes of Kievan Rus. Vladimir, a leader of this feudal state, brought Christianity to Russia in 988 and, legend says, baptized his 12 sons in the brook that flowed through the valley.

A thousand years later, the Ukrainian capital is again green, with half its area in woods, parks, and gardens. In spring, blooming chestnut trees line Kreshchatyk and the other streets of a city almost completely rebuilt following some of World War II's worst devastation.

99

Although Soviet people sometimes say, "We have no war memorials, only peace memorials," war has often been the fate of Ukraine. In Kiev, statuary and a great arch commemorate the reunification in 1654 of Ukraine and the Russian state after centuries of Mongol invasion and foreign domination. At a reunion, World War II veterans honor their comrades and the five million Ukrainians who died during the war and the three-year Nazi occupation. The major general's sash proclaims him an honorary citizen of Donetsk. Above all his other medals he wears the plain gold star of a Hero of the Soviet Union.

T he dedication of Kiev's Cathedral of St. Sophia (above, left) in 1037 signaled a golden era of Christian culture and power. Its builder, Prince Vladimir's son Yaroslav, modeled it after the Hagia Sophia in Constantinople. Beyond architecture and art, the princes of Kiev emulated the Byzantine example in education, literature, and language, sponsoring the Cyrillic alphabet used, ever since, by Russians and Ukrainians.

Kiev also imported from Eastern Orthodoxy the sacred chant and response, unaccompanied by instruments, as well as baptism, marriage, holy orders, and other sacraments.

103

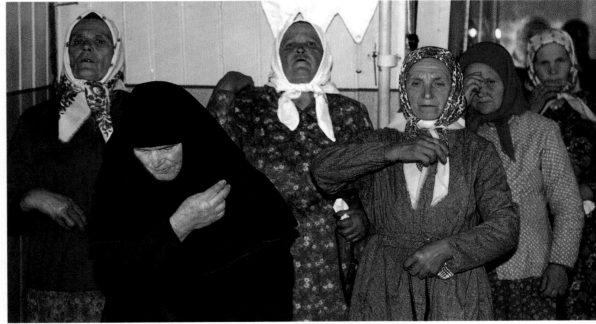

The sacramental rites of Russian churches confirm a sense of community, or *sobornost, a* centuries-old cultural value so profound that *sobor came to* mean "cathedral."

On a holy day at St. Vladimir's Cathedral in Kiev, Russian Orthodox priests bless food that worshipers have brought from home and will take back for family meals thus consecrated to God.

The Russian women in Moldavia (above) are Old Believers, a group that broke from the established church in the 17th century, objecting to changes in liturgy and ritual. Among other practices, Old Believers retained the newly forbidden two-fingered sign of the cross—to them a symbol of Christ's dual nature, both human and divine.

Millions of Old Believers, often severely persecuted, created communal, pietistic settlements all across Russian territory and beyond, in a flight that scholars compare to the exodus of the Puritans to New England.

105

I n the Moldavian village of Kunicha, Old Believers hold a community wedding for three couples. The parents of one groom (above, top) welcome guests with an icon and the traditional sign of hospitality, bread and salt.

The ancestors of these people settled here in 1723, fleeing reprisals in the Moscow region. Old Believers have always been known as sober, disciplined, hardworking, generally prosperous people. Historians count their absence from mainstream Russian life a great loss, especially to the Russian Orthodox Church which, weakened by the schism, turned for support to the state.

L enin presides at the Kiev Central Wedding Palace (opposite). When a bride and groom enter the marriage hall, they will make their vows in a state ritual as fixed as any religious ceremony.

After a brief series of questions on the duties of a Soviet family, they are man and wife, and with family and witnesses they leave the chamber to make way for the next couple. Especially on Saturdays, wedding palaces see a steady turnover.

The wedding party, by custom, proceeds to a monument or historical site, where they will have pictures taken and the bride will leave flowers. Each city has its favored destinations: in Moscow, Lenin's Mausoleum or the Flame of the Unknown Soldier. In Yalta, it may be Swallow's Nest (left), a villa built in 1912 by a German oil baron who called it his Castle of Love.

109

A patina of age mellows a street in the old center of Lvov, a city cherished by Ukrainians as a fountainhead of their culture. Founded in the 13th century by a Ukrainian prince, Lvov became one of medieval Europe's greatest trading centers, and a prize dominated, over its history, by Poland, Austria-Hungary, Germany, and Russia. Ethnic and religious diversity have long marked Lvov and western Ukraine, but Ukrainian tradition and language have been kept alive by renowned educational institutions and a strong spirit of nationalism.

111

T ruth and illusion compete in Odessa. Posters appeal for glasnost 100%; for honesty about Stalin's crimes; and for truth—pravda—unvarnished.

Fantasy reigns just blocks away, where a turn-of-the-century hotel becomes a movie set. Until government repression began in 1930, studios in Odessa, Kiev, and other Ukrainian cities produced motion pictures with national themes. Film historians rank some Ukrainian films among the greatest ever made.

T heir day's work done, Donetsk coal miners clean up from labors in a tunnel half a mile underground, where a worker (above) telephones to the surface. Hundreds of mines honeycomb the Donets basin, 22 of them under the city of Donetsk. Though Donets output is declining, the mines produce a third of the USSR's coal.

Pages 116-117: A port has existed at Odessa, on the Black Sea, since ancient times. It began to thrive in the 18th century, after military expansion by Catherine the Great. Today Odessa and its next-door twin port, Ilichevsk, are the busiest in the nation.

Tiny new citizens lie swaddled at Maternity House #2 in Chernovtsy, Ukraine. At the age of 10 days, they will go home with their mothers, who receive state-paid maternity leave of 56 days before the baby's birth and 56 days afterward.

Before long most will join a kindergarten (detsky sad—a children's garden) or a day-care group such as these Kiev toddlers out for a walk.

Millions of Soviet youngsters, some as young as five, belong to chess clubs. In Yalta, children maneuver intently, timed by a bell that will announce the end of one game and the beginning of another. For more than a thousand years, Russians have played chess. The Bolsheviks adopted it as a "tool of intellectual culture," and the state heaps honor on chess masters, of whom the USSR has more than any other nation in the world.

119

H olidaymakers enjoy magic shows and horror shows at an amusement park (above, top) in Kishinev, Moldavia. A warm sun draws others to Yalta, on the Black Sea. Yalta's latitude—44°N—puts it as far north as Bangor, Maine, but it lies in an amphitheater, wrapped by mountains that block north winds and create a setting that has charmed Russians and foreigners since the 19th century. Today the villas and palaces of tsarist days are museums or workers' sanitoriums, and Yalta's hotels and boardinghouses every year host millions of vacationers and health seekers, drawn to blue skies and the sea.

The Caucasus

By Jon Thompson
Photographs by George F. Mobley

The peaks of the Caucasus are seldom more than 50 miles from the plains as the crow flies, but in these mountains even crows do not fly in straight lines, and the peaks must be reached by traveling up the river valleys. The typical valley has the shape of a spoon; low down it fans out but, as you ascend, it narrows like the spoon's handle. Here, a river becomes a furious torrent confined by steeply rising cliffs which make access difficult and sometimes perilous. Farther up, the valley opens out like the bowl of the spoon, and large areas may be suitable for grazing or agriculture. This shape makes for inaccessibility and easy defense, and throughout the ages people fleeing from the endless struggles and wars for the fertile lowlands have found refuge in these secluded valleys.

In the last century the mountainous Caucasus was still a dangerous region where men went about armed and banditry was considered a noble vocation. It was little known by Westerners then, and remains so to this day.

Although the Scythians, Romans, Byzantines, Arabs, Khazars, Mongols, Persians, and Turks had all conquered parts of the Caucasus in their heyday, the forces of imperial Russia were the first to control the entire region. By the 1860s the conquest and pacification of the Caucasus, which had taken more than 60 years of desperate fighting, was more or less complete. As soon as it became safe to travel, foreign mountaineers, turning their attention from the Alps to the more lofty Caucasian peaks, began to explore. The books they wrote about their adventures provide some of the few early descriptions of the Caucasus made by foreigners. As travelers' tales so often do, they speak of the miserable conditions in the villages, the poverty of the local inhabitants, their rough manners and dress, and the lack of variety in their diet. But they were full of praise for the human qualities of the mountain people, admiring especially their loyalty, honor, respect for tradition, warlike spirit, and fierce independence.

That brief window on the Caucasus closed in 1919 with the Russian Revolution and Civil War. It reopened for a few years in the late 1920s, and finally slammed shut in 1930 with Stalin's liquidation of the "rich peasants"—the kulaks—and destruction of private-enterprise agriculture by the forced collectivization of farmlands. World War II heaped disaster on an already suffering country, and the Caucasus has, in effect, remained closed for Westerners ever since—except for the main cities and a few well-trodden official tourist routes. Only recently has travel in rural areas again become possible.

Look at a map and you will see how the Caucasus Mountains rise abruptly

Detail of a dagger scabbard from Georgia, in gold, silver, and enamel-like niello work.

out of the great plains of European Russia and stretch for 750 miles in a long straight line running roughly east-west between the Black Sea and the Caspian. They form a great wall between the open steppe to the north and the complex mixture of peoples and territories to the south. The foothills and lowlands are a natural paradise. The valley of the great Kuban River, northwest of the mountains, struck me—who grew up on a farm—as particularly beautiful, with its deep, rich alluvial soil, abundant water, deciduous forest, gentle hills, and wildflowers everywhere. Throughout history it has been envied, fought over, and occupied by many different peoples, as its rich archaeological remains reveal.

To the south lie the prolific lands of Georgia, Armenia, and Azerbaijan, known as the Transcaucasus. Here, territorial boundaries echo the ancient division of the region between the Roman and Persian Empires; Christian Armenia and Georgia incline historically westward, whereas Muslim Azerbaijan looks eastward to Persia for its cultural connections. The Transcaucasus is a region where culture flourished in parallel with the achievements of its ancient, great neighbors of western Europe and the Near East.

The high valleys are surprisingly fertile—wheat ripens at 6,700 feet, twice as high as in the Alps—and people living in them can be more or less self-supporting. Such isolated communities, scattered throughout the Caucasus, are touched slowly by the changing currents of taste and fashion in the lowlands. In these remote habitats the rarest cultural forms still flourish, a last refuge for languages and traditions which died long ago in the mainstream of civilization.

I came across an interesting survival one day at the source of the Terek, the river of the north Caucasus which flows northward through Ossetia and then eastward to the Caspian. It rises in Georgia in a high valley inhabited by a few families of shepherds. A difficult and dangerous single-track dirt road, suitable only for four-wheel-drive vehicles, winds up a narrow gorge with a sheer drop to the fierce torrent below. The valley, flanked by the snowy peaks around Mount Kazbek, opens out amidst a tumble of red rocks to a broad plain covered with alpine flowers. The rocks add a rusty color to the river where a hot spring bubbles up with deep blue water. To the left great sheets of white tumble down the hillside where a mineral-laden spring deposits its salts. In the distance tall, partly ruined stone towers stand in commanding positions. I watched the play of light on a huge flock of sheep moving across a steep slope.

It began to rain hard and my driver thought it best to leave. On the way down through a narrow gorge, at a particularly difficult section of the road, two trucks blocked the way. We reversed and maneuvered ourselves off the road and, as the rain stopped, waited for them to advance. Nothing happened, so I went to find out what was going on. Drawing near, I found four men standing before a small fissure in the black rock at a bend of the road. They were unshaven and dressed in nondescript brown or gray trousers, shirts, and dull-colored sweaters or windbreakers. Their arms were raised in an attitude of prayer. Although the roar of the river drowned all sounds, I could see they were singing. Not liking to interrupt, I waited at a respectful distance until they had finished, when they promptly jumped into their two trucks.

"This is a holy place," one driver explained as they drove past me, "and you must always stop and drink a little. Then your journey will be easy." They roared off along the track at what seemed an incredibly dangerous speed, honking their horns as they went. Where they had stopped was an immense accumulation of empty bottles, neatly stacked, a huge jar of homemade liquor, half full, some bread, and pieces of cooked lamb. This was clearly a food offering to a local deity. The liquor tasted very good and I was surprised on the way down to find myself spending less time than I had on the way up pressing my imaginary brake pedal and leaning away from the stomach-churning precipice.

Local gods and spirits are still very much alive in North Ossetia. Most Ossetians are nominally Christian but the practices of the Christian world lie lightly atop their old beliefs. In the village of Dargavs, in the upper valley of the Gizeldon River, I found the old deities faithfully remembered in elaborate toasting rituals. The people are infinitely hospitable, and issue invitations to eat and drink on sight. The old books mention a kind of beer which is still made, but that is not good enough for a distinguished foreigner! Out comes the vodka or cognac, and unseen but very real powers are called to memory, one after another. The deities are not anthropomorphic but natural forces evident to us all: the power of a tree to bear fruit, of a field to give harvest, of a woman to produce children, of invisible elements to protect or harm a traveler.

In a Khevsur village, in a high valley in Georgia, I was tidying away some uneaten food after a picnic. We had stopped near a small, dilapidated, windowless, gray stone building, surrounded by a ruined stone wall. In front of the little building stood a low stone arch with a bell. Near the wall lay upside down two riveted copper cauldrons. Such cauldrons, scholars say, are used for beer in feast-day rituals. The technique looked medieval to me but the cauldrons that I saw were not cast away or abandoned—no weeds grew up around them.

As I began to put away the remainders of our meal, a villager spoke to me. "You must leave it where it is," he said, "because we are on holy ground." The building was their church, supposedly Christian, but the cauldrons spoke of something other than the usual Christian ceremonies. I left my offering.

The mysterious Khevsurs are an ancient people with their own language and ways who live in the most inaccessible high valleys of Georgia. I was allowed to photograph the small building and its bell but strictly forbidden to enter. There still is much to be learned from people such as the Khevsurs, among whom beliefs, customs, and language change only slowly. Today, roads, radio, television, education, and military service all bring the modern world closer, and soon the lingering traces of the ancient world will vanish altogether.

In former times the valleys supported a much larger population than they do now and more land was under cultivation. In practically every valley terraced hillsides once used for agriculture are now given over to grazing, or are overgrown with young forest. Dead townships in several valleys also bear witness to a dramatic drop in the population of centuries ago. Heaps of gray stones covered with green and orange lichens scattered over a hillside are all that remain of the village of Kundup, near Nalchik, on the northern edge of the mountains. There is no sign of fire or destruction; the abandoned village is just crumbling away. Nearby are curious catacombs littered with skeletons. Local people say that several villages in the valley were wiped out by plague and that people with the disease took themselves off, crawled into the catacombs, lay down, and died.

Today the population of the Caucasus is exploding. In Khurik, a Dagestan village populated by members of the Tabasaran ethnic group—a beautiful, friendly people—there were so many children that most of the girls were carrying and looking after little ones. The mayor invited me to dine with him in the home of a man who had sought the honor of playing host. At the house we took off our shoes and climbed a stairway to the second floor. It is the custom for the men to eat together while the women cook and serve. We sat down to a laden table—the mayor, the inevitable party official, the host and his son, my driver, and I. The host's granddaughter served, speaking to us in English. There was a garlic-flavored vegetable soup, grilled mutton, lamb kebabs, yogurt, cheese with fresh herbs, tomatoes, and great quantities of bread freshly baked in a wood-burning stove.

The mayor handed me a portion of the Tabasaran national dish, a kind of pancake filled with chopped lamb. "It is good for male potency," he declared matter-of-factly. "We need it because the Tabasaran population is falling. In the old days women had 15 children, now they have only 12."

I had my doubts about his claim and later I looked up the figures. Between 1970 and 1979 the Tabasaran population rose by an astonishing 36.4 percent, while the Russian population grew by only 6.5 percent in the same period. A ban on the consumption of lamb-filled pancakes might be a first move in warding off the fast-approaching overpopulation problem.

In the past, the principal means of population control seems to have been warfare. Tribes, clans, villages, even families were perpetually fighting each other. Vendettas were conducted according to an elaborate set of rules and could continue for several generations. Villages were built in easily defended places and equipped with tall, tapering, four-cornered stone refuge towers which were also used as lookouts. These towers are a feature of village architecture in the high valleys throughout the central Caucasus on both sides of the mountains.

I explored a tower in Chechenia. Access was through a small opening with a stout wooden door about 10 feet from the ground. In the old days it was reached by a ladder drawn up by the last person to enter. The door opened onto a room some 12 feet square, vaulted with massive curved stones. There was a large wooden grain chest made of planks fashioned with an adze. Access to the upper stories was via a small hole in the ceiling, again by ladder. Near the top of the 60-foot tower small windows and arrow slits faced in four directions. The Pax Russica has removed the need for these towers and most have fallen into ruin.

Today's population increase has created a construction boom. The old houses—now almost a thing of the past—were built of stone and timber. They had a flat roof of rammed earth and grit, used for sleeping under the stars, socializing, drying fruit, and miscellaneous household tasks. The new houses are built with manufactured materials. Clusters of harsh white roofs—made from sheets of corrugated asbestos cement—now disfigure the landscape.

In the last 20 years, the living standard has risen throughout the Caucasus, and the way of life has changed with it. Some places described by travelers a hundred years ago are recognizable only by their name. Roads have been built where only horses could go before, and a three-day journey is made in three hours now. Virtually every village has electricity, with parades of poles and festoons of ugly wires. The trappings of modern life—television, plastic bags, factory-made clothes—penetrate everywhere. Progress it may be, but I was often saddened by the lack of sympathy between these new-style villages and the timeless beauty of nature all around them. Yet I know there is no going back; who but a crank would be without electricity and the telephone if there were a choice?

The new houses are large by any standards, and palatial compared to the tiny apartments city dwellers throughout the Soviet Union are forced to live in. Caucasian village life compares favorably to city life in other ways, too. This came home to me when I visited a family in a mountain village in Balkaria. The first surprise was hearing them speak a form of Turkish, a language I always associate with pastures and open grazing rather than forested mountains. The reason for the anomaly is a classic one. The Balkars are the remnants of a once mighty nomadic people driven into the mountains from the steppe by the Mongols in the 13th century. Here, in isolation, they have retained their language for 700 years. The second surprise was their income. The mother and two daughters blended sheep's wool and cashmere, dyed it, and knitted it into sweaters. They also made soft, open-work woolen scarves on a knitting machine. The average income in the Soviet Union is about 220 rubles per month; they admitted to earning 1,000 rubles per month, which means they almost certainly earn more.

The history of the Balkars is known but the origin of most of the Caucasian peoples is a mystery. The neighboring Ossetians, like the Balkars, know their history; they are descendants of a once great nomadic people, the Alans, and speak a language closely related to Persian. But in the Caucasus these matters are never simple. Attempts to discover something of the lost history of the Caucasian peoples by studying their languages have had little success. A linguist from Moscow told me that the Caucasian languages are unrelated to any of the languages of Europe, Asia, or the Far East. They form an entire language family of their own and must have developed in isolation over a very long period.

The number and diversity of languages in the Caucasus is astonishing. In Dagestan alone, 32 separate languages are spoken, of which some, Avar for example, have a number of distinct dialects each understood in only a single valley. When traveling I always try to learn a few words of the local language, but I came unstuck in the Caucasus. The richness of strange consonants produced by a Lak speaker or an Avar is hard to imagine. I was told by a Tabasaran that his language has 53 consonants. The word for "good-bye" in Khevsur was so strange that I could not begin to imitate it. Several languages are still unwritten and barely studied (Tsakhur, Agul, and Rutul, for instance), and there are even languages spoken only within a single village; Andi and Kubachi, to name two.

In appearance the people are as varied as their languages. Azerbaijanis are usually swarthy with black wavy hair. In Dagestan some extremely striking physical types can be found, especially among those communities with the custom of marrying only within their clan. Twice, once in Ossetia and again in Dagestan, I met local people who could tell a person's village from his or her features. Blue-eyed people and redheads can also be found among the indigenous population of the valleys, as indeed they can in all the high mountainous regions of western Asia. The suggestion that this trait has something to do with the troops of Alexander of Macedon is an oft-repeated fiction copied by one author from another. On a beach near Makhachkala, on Dagestan's Caspian coast, I was expecting my light skin to stand out. On the contrary, although the majority of people in Dagestan have brown eyes and hair, fair skins predominate.

The greatest linguistic diversity occurs in Dagestan. Although the mountains there are not so high as in the central Caucasus, they are more spread out. Dagestan's terrain is broken and difficult; not even bulldozers and dynamite have made travel easy there. It took nine hours of hard driving to reach Botlikh in the heart of Avar territory, and when I made the same journey (in 40 minutes) in a single-engine biplane it was easy to see why. The rivers have worn great canyons through the countryside. Erosion is on a vast scale; grassy highlands are interrupted by steep drops to a riverbed; craggy islands project at random from its floor and wooded slopes give way to soaring rock faces. There is no easy route anywhere. The valleys here are much longer than in the central Caucasus. The Samur River Valley of southern Dagestan, for example, where the unwritten Tsakhur, Agul, and Rutul are spoken, is 125 miles long. Though broad, open, and not difficult to enter, it offers few prospects to the potential invader because in the interior there are neither large areas of arable land nor sizable towns.

Dagestan villages are built in the most inaccessible places, and houses tumble down the hillsides rather than clustering as they do in the central Caucasus. The towers of the central Caucasian villages are mostly absent here, except in border zones. Cereal crops, grapevines, and potatoes grow in patches. Fruit trees abound—Dagestan apricots are famous—and almonds and hazelnuts are important in the diet, as are cheese and yogurt. The cows are usually kept in a part of the house. Chickens are everywhere. There are huge flocks of sheep that belong to collectives and smaller flocks of "private" sheep.

It was in the rugged terrain of north Dagestan and the Chechen-Ingush Republic that the Russians experienced the greatest resistance in their conquest of the Caucasus. There the great Imam Shamil, leader of the Muslim fraternity of Murids, held out against the Russians for almost 30 years after the rest of the

Caucasus had been conquered. Shamil was so respected as a warrior that when he finally surrendered in 1859 the tsar was moved to give him a house and a pension. But to this day, the Murids' hearts and minds remain unconquered.

I gained insight into the present feelings of some north Caucasian Muslims when I visited a Chechen friend, Magomet. When foreigners are invited into a home, it often happens that the normal rules and customs are relaxed for their benefit. Not so with Magomet; the old patriarchal traditions were inflexible. At table (men only, of course) the head of the household reigned supreme. He acted as general master of ceremonies and decided when those present might speak or smoke. Magomet and his family are fervent Muslims, although he is a member of the Communist Party. But his witty and cynical comments revealed clearly what he really felt. I particularly liked his description of communism: the triumph of Marxism and Leninism over common sense.

During the meal, Magomet told me about the turbulent history of his people. He spoke calmly but intensely. "In 1943," he said, "the German forces were approaching the Caucasus in their advance toward the rich oil fields around Baku. Stalin was afraid that some of the mountain people would turn their guns on Russians instead of Germans, so he ordered the deportation of the entire Chechen, Ingush, Karachai, and Balkar populations, together with some other Muslim peoples. Our men, women, and children, plus whatever possessions they could carry, were bundled into trucks, seven families in each, and taken to Kazakhstan and Central Asia. They were given only a few hours notice. Many people died from starvation and exposure on the way. Life was hard and altogether we lost about a quarter of our people. My grandmother was shot during the journey because she wanted to go to the toilet. My brother and I were born in Kazakhstan. In 1968 we were all allowed to return, but my family was unlucky. Other people had moved into our village and destroyed the cemetery."

In the regions where Shamil fought his famous battles the people remain strongly religious; the passion of the newly converted, perhaps, because the Sunni branch of Islam came to this part of the north Caucasus only in the 18th century. Their fervor is matched by the almost religious intensity of the efforts made by the Soviet authorities to stamp out Islam. For instance, in 1943 all the mosques and religious colleges in Chechen-Ingushetia, over 1,200 of them, were closed at a stroke (and most still are). A great campaign to spread "scientific atheism," the official religion of the Communist Party, was launched. The effect has been zero. The people are as devout as ever and an extensive network of secret Sufi brotherhoods operates very effectively without the need for mosques. The ham-handed efforts of the authorities to suppress Islam act as a continuous provocation and give strength to already powerful anticommunist and anti-Russian feelings which can and do erupt into violence.

Several times my travel plans in the USSR have been altered at the last minute by civil unrest. In 1988 it was Baku, when martial law was imposed to quell riots over the disputed territory of Nagorno Karabakh. In May 1989 it was Tbilisi where 20 people were killed and hundreds injured when crack combat troops recently out of Afghanistan were flown in to break up an anti-Russian demonstration. When I heard about the brutality of the troops against the Georgians, I remembered how the Russians came to be in Georgia in the first place. In 1801 the kingdom of Georgia, having for years suffered invasions from Turkey, Persia, and Russia, found itself in a perilous position. The king, believing that the best future lay with Russia, petitioned the tsar, asking that the kingdom of Georgia become a Russian protectorate. The Russian reply was to annex Georgia and abolish the monarchy. The tsar's manifesto is couched in terms which have become all too familiar: It was not to extend the borders of the largest empire in the world, the manifesto claimed, but humanity in response to the prayers of the suffering people of Georgia. It concluded that the profits and prosperity of Georgia would be the tsar's sole reward. After these sweet words the Russians used Georgia as a bridgehead for colonizing the rest of the Caucasus.

It has become unfashionable to talk of great powers and their colonies, but that is exactly how some people in the Caucasus see their relationship to Moscow even today. In Azerbaijan an academician told me that the major part of their oil and wool is exported to other parts of the Soviet Union as raw material. This arrangement deprives Azerbaijan of the income it would have if the materials were processed within the republic. The idea of a colony supplying raw materials to its "mother country" seemed a perfectly natural one in the 18th and 19th centuries, but looks outdated in the 20th.

The subject peoples of what used to be the Russian Empire are reassessing their relationship to Moscow. Ethnic Russians in the republics are in an increasingly hostile environment, and for the last ten years they have been leaving Azerbaijan and Georgia. The prospect of the Russian Empire falling apart may give its enemies pleasure, but the thought of what would happen to the Caucasian people if Soviet power left the Caucasus is terrifying and could make the civil war in Lebanon look like a minor squabble. We have the prospect of the Ossetians fighting among themselves, the Chechens fighting the Dagestanis, the Armenians the Azerbaijanis, and the Abkhazians the Georgians. In each republic there would be pro-Russian and anti-Russian factions at each other's throats. Imagine Armenia under fire from both Turkey and Azerbaijan at the same time, Azerbaijan under threat of invasion by Iran, and Turkey demanding the return of parts of Georgia. Without some strong stabilizing influence in the area, the Caucasus could destroy itself in perpetual warfare.

I asked Magomet what he thought about the future, but should have known better. He grimaced. "In my father's day," he said, "Shamil was praised by the Communists as a hero fighting for the liberation of his people from the tsar's imperialist yoke. When I was a boy this was all changed. The tsarist troops were the heroes; they liberated the mountain people from the clerical tyranny of Shamil, who was a stooge of the British and Turkish imperialists. In a country where even the past is unpredictable, only God can know the future."

T he green slopes of the Caucasus Mountains surround Tanzatap, a hamlet in Armenia, the smallest of the Soviet Republics. The region of the Caucasus and Transcaucasus includes Armenia, Georgia, Azerbaijan, Dagestan—in all, some ten political divisions. It is marked by geographic complexity and largely rigorous terrain ranging from highmountain glaciers to belowsea-level salt marshes. Despite such obstacles, the region became an invasion and migration bridge between eastern Europe and the Near East as early as the seventh century B.C. Some 50 distinct peoples of Caucasus villages, towns, and mountain valleys speak as many as 83 languages and dialects, many ancient. The Roman army, while conducting business here in the first century B.C., needed 80 interpreters, according to Pliny the Elder.

H andwoven carpets patterned from memory or from sketches are sold at the Sunday morning bazaar in Derbent, Dagestan. The wall in the background formed part of a fifth-century citadel that guarded the narrow coastal passage between the Caspian Sea and the eastern spurs of the Caucasus. This vital route attracted hordes of conquering Arabs, Mongols, Persians, and Turks. Derbent, "barrier" in Persian, appears in signature on the bottom of a carpet woven in traditional style, at a modern factory.

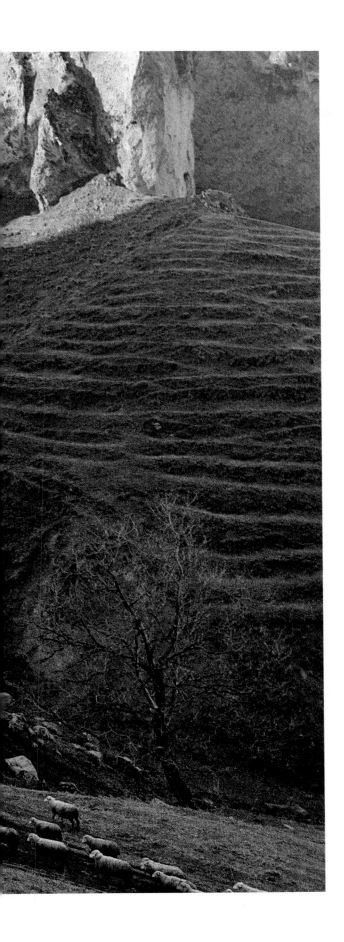

A variety of climates and landscapes means a variety of work for rural people. Livestock find ideal pasture in alpine meadows southwest of Goris, Armenia. Tea plantations (above, top) lie in the subtropical lowlands of the Lenkoran district of Azerbaijan, where village elders congregate daily.

Pages 136-137: Mount Ararat towers above Yerevan, Armenia. The biblical resting place of Noah's ark, the mountain stands across the border in Turkey, 40 miles from the city. Armenians hold it sacred, believing themselves descended from the first race to appear after the Flood.

135

I
n Baku, capital of Azerbaijan, senior citizens perform early morning calisthenics. They work out in a "health zone," an area where, under medical supervision, people follow therapeutic exercise and diet designed to deter aging. Azerbaijan, famous for the longevity of its people, claims some 45 centenarians for every 100,000 citizens.

The roofs of 15th-century baths in the walled Old City testify to the legacy of health in Baku. The baths were sunk into the ground for coolness in summer and warmth in winter. They used steam and cold dips to cleanse the body and ease muscular aches.

139

A rtist Rasim Ganifa Ogli Babayev displays paintings at his gallery in Baku. His interpretive style of blending fantasy with reality emerged in the 1960s and is steeped in the legends and mythology of his native Azerbaijan. His bright, rich colors reflect those found in other Azerbaijani arts such as pottery and rug weaving.

On a spring Sunday in Tbilisi, Georgia, the cornucopia of gardens and orchards spills forth at the central market while, in a riverside park across town, craftsmen and artists sell their works. Georgia's Mediterranean climate allows for lemon, orange, and tangerine groves, herbs, vineyards and famous wines, tea plantations, nuts, mushrooms—a bounty of fresh fruits and vegetables all year long—and a wealth and warmth of hospitality and culture known the world around.

143

T bilisi sparkles in enveloping dusk. The Kura River, witness to the history of the region, rises in Turkey, flows through the heart of Tbilisi, and empties into the Caspian Sea 340 miles from the city.

Built as a fortress in the 4th century, Tbilisi suffered centuries of conquerors, enjoyed a flourishing court in the 12th century, then endured more invasions. In 1795 a Persian army razed most of the city. Today the ambience of this capital of Georgia mingles Tatar wooden balconies on old houses, Turkish baths, Oriental bazaars, 4th-century battlements, minarets, churches founded more than a thousand years ago, 19th-century boulevards, and a 20th-century bronze Lenin who stands in the shadow of the mountains that ring the city.

144

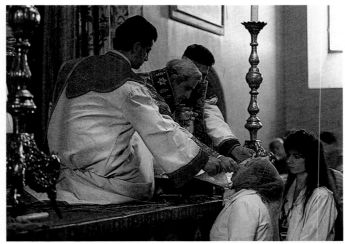

I n the seventh-century Echmiadzin Cathedral, Catholicos Vazgen I attends Mass (left and above, top). Since the 14th century, Echmiadzin has been the capital and the residence of the patriarch of the Armenian Apostolic Church. Chief among the religions of the Caucasus are Islam, Judaism, Eastern Orthodoxy, and Armenian Christianity.

Bells frame the Sveti Tskhoveli Cathedral, an example of 15th-century Georgian architecture in Mtskheta. A seat of the Georgian Orthodox Church, the cathedral dedicated to the Twelve Apostles was, until 1800, the site of the coronation of Georgian kings.

147

A young couple, having tied a wish to a branch, emerges from a sea of handkerchief-knotted trees at the Gueghard Monastery in Armenia. The vaulted, candle-lit main church of the monastery (above) was built in the 13th century, and is one of four churches hewn from the solid rock hills. A famous spiritual and cultural center of medieval Armenia, Gueghard, "lance" in Armenian, is named for the spearhead thought to have pierced Christ on the cross, once kept here and now in the Echmiadzin Cathedral.

M oonlight glistens on the Caspian over one of the USSR's richest seafloor oil fields. Near Baku, workers relax in a dormitory of Neftyanye Kamni—"oil rocks"—a town and oil extraction complex built on steel pilings and suspended above the waves off the Apsheron Peninsula, a spur of the Caucasus extending 50 miles into the Caspian. Some 6,000 people of 27 different nationalities work here in shifts—a week or two on the rocks, then equal time for shore leave.

152

AIR&SPACE
Smithsonian

Enter my membership in the National Air & Space Museum, including a year of *AIR & SPACE/Smithsonian* (6 issues).

☐ Bill me $18. ☐ Bill me at the reduced rate of $16. I am a Smithsonian Associate, Contributing, Resident Associate, or Cooper-Hewitt Member.

Name _____

Address _____

City _____

State, Zip _____

5SB33

MEMBERSHIP BENEFITS

- *AIR & SPACE/Smithsonian* magazine (6 issues)
- Book and gift discounts from Museum shops and by mail
- Reduced rates for special Museum IMAX films and Planetarium shows
- Eligibility for travel programs
- Members' welcome at the Museum

Please add $6.00 dues for foreign orders and prepay in U.S. funds. 85% of dues is designated for magazine subscription. Please allow 4-6 weeks to receive your first copy of *AIR & SPACE/Smithsonian*.

BUSINESS REPLY MAIL

FIRST CLASS   PERMIT NO. 1269   BOULDER, CO.

POSTAGE WILL BE PAID BY ADDRESSEE

National Air & Space Museum
Smithsonian Institution
Membership-Subscription Center
P.O. Box 51244
Boulder, Co. 80321-1244

A model of the product manufactured at the Baku Deepwater Platform Station stands behind a gardener ready to till the field. When these deep-sea platforms, weighing up to 20,000 tons each, leave the factory (above), dump barges transport them to drill sites as much as 70 miles by sea from Baku. The oil fields of the Apsheron Peninsula were exploited in the 1870s, and by 1900 Baku supplied half the world's oil. Fortunes were made and the largest fields belonged to foreign companies like Nobel and Rothschild. Today production is falling but Baku excels in petrochemical research and technology.

153

Children play among leaning headstones in a Muslim cemetery outside Derbent. The 18th-century grave markers often have inscriptions from the Koran and symbols corresponding to the sex of the deceased—guns and horses for men, flowers and birds for women.

In the Caucasus, ancient religious ways persist, mingling with Islam and Christianity. In Dargavs, an Ossetian City of the Dead built from the 14th to the 19th century, houses in the living village each had a corresponding mausoleum. The dead, dressed in their best, were laid out to mummify, supplied with possessions for a happy afterlife.

Kazakhstan & Central Asia

By Geoffrey Moorhouse
Photographs by Nicole Bengiveno

he young Orthodox priest gestured toward the snowbound blankness beyond the edge of town and shrugged in resignation. "It just goes on and on, world without end, amen," he said, "and I know that one day soon I shall be defeated by it. I shall have to get out." We were in Tselinograd, in northern Kazakhstan, and he was referring to the flatness of the steppe, which stretched away for unimaginable distances on every side. Himself a Ukrainian from gently rolling and compact country beside the River Don, he had been unable to come to terms with the immensity of the landscape out there. It intimidated him.

The fact is that he could have gone nowhere in that part of the Soviet Union to escape being overwhelmed by its topography. Kazakhstan is four times the size of Texas and includes a lot of bleak and empty flatland, which is one reason why the Soviet nuclear testing ground is established there, as well as the takeoff and landing sites for cosmonauts. Add to it the republics of Kirghizia, Uzbekistan, Turkmenia, and Tajikistan (the smallest of them, about the size of Florida) and you have the extent of Soviet Central Asia. Virtually a subcontinent whose natural features are, without exception, gigantic.

What is not steppe in Central Asia is often semidesert or desert, most notably the Kyzyl Kum of Uzbekistan, the Kara Kum of Turkmenia, the Betpak Dala of Kazakhstan. In some places dunes rise 300 feet high. And when these variously sandy or grassy, mostly flat lands finally expire, it is because they have run up against range after range of mountains which barricade the nation against its neighbors to the south. Separating Turkmenia from Iran are cliffs which might be crossed after a hard day's climbing, but farther east the barricade becomes much higher. The Pamirs and the Tian Shan rise sensationally in that corner of the globe where the Soviet Union, Afghanistan, Pakistan, India, and China converge. Here is the so-called roof of the world, thousands of square miles in which few of the peaks are less than 20,000 feet. The icy summits gleam entrancingly, rank after rank of them, when the sun shines on their vertical sides, their ridges, and their pinnacles; but at all other times they are utterly forbidding.

If you fly over the area you become aware of the force that lies below the surface of those heights. Huge thicknesses of rock lie folded like furrows across the landscape, the product of that phenomenon geologists know as the India-Eurasian Collision. The subcontinent of India is gradually shifting northward, pressing ineluctably against the even greater mass of Eurasia with such energy that the mountains between are being squeezed upward—are increasing in

A *tyubeteika*, traditional Central Asian skullcap of velvet, cotton, and gold embroidery.

height—by about an inch every five years. Regular earthquakes, a result of the stress of those folds, terribly change the very contours of the world.

Places that have been ruined by earthquake include Alma Ata, where all but one house was destroyed in 1887; Ashkhabad, almost wiped out in 1948; and Tashkent, the fourth largest city in the Soviet Union, which lost one-third of its buildings in 1966. Nothing can be constructed in this precarious region without taking the possibility of earthquake into account. When hydroelectric engineers needed to dam a tributary of the Amu Darya—the Vakhsh, at Nurek in Tajikistan—they did not build the enormous buttress in ferroconcrete. Instead, in the early 1970s, Nurek became the world's highest dam of earth and loose rock, built that way in order to absorb shock waves without crumbling as a rigid structure might. It towers 1,033 feet above the bottom of its gorge, where it is almost a mile thick, holding back the deepest artificial lake yet made; which, were it to be suddenly released, would imperil 30,000 people in the town just below the dam, and other small towns downstream from Nurek.

The earthquakes are not always spectacular, as I discovered in the Tajik village of Sharora, a couple of weeks after it had suffered catastrophe in the wake of the Armenian disaster of 1988. In Tajikistan there had been no sudden tremor collapsing buildings. Instead, the earthquake had sent a tide of mud sliding inexorably down a low hillside in the early morning. The tide had simply engulfed Sharora, stealthily, while many of the villagers slept; and where at last it had come to a standstill, it had oozed into another home, whose roof and upper walls were still visible. Everything on the gentle slope above had been obliterated. Men wearing Tajik skullcaps, often in long quilted coats with vivid stripes, stood looking down on the sea of mud, now patched with fresh snow. Beneath it were crushed homes and 274 of their dead. A horseman, clad in purple with a yellow cummerbund, rode up and stared inscrutably at this mass grave before trotting off again. No, it was not spectacular but it was very, very final.

It is and always has been a struggle to wrest sustenance from this territory. In 1954 northern Kazakhstan saw the beginning of the Virgin and Long Idle Lands program, whose purpose was at one and the same time to make the steppe more than a vast pasture for seminomadic people and their herds of sheep and horses; and to help solve the nation's perennial shortage of land cultivated for grain. In the initial years an area greater than the arable acreage of France, West Germany, and the United Kingdom combined was put to the plow and drilled for cereals. But the average rainfall is under 16 inches a year and the cultivators soon encountered problems familiar to farmers in the American Midwest—dust storms, erosion, and the like. It's a quarter of a century now since any significant new virgin lands were plowed up in Kazakhstan, where most of the steppe still lies empty of anything but its traditional grazing herds.

There's been more success in bringing life to the Kara Kum, which covers more than 115,000 square miles of Turkmenia. The name translates from Turkic as "black sands" but this refers to danger, not color, for in strong sunlight the sand appears nearly white. This is conventional desert, with dunes formed by the winds that sweep it almost ceaselessly, and small herds of camels.

An impressive transformation has happened here, due to the cutting of the Kara Kum Canal, which is reckoned to be more than twice as long as the Suez, Panama, Kiel, North Sea, Corinth, and Manchester Ship Canals combined. By the start of 1989 it had reached just beyond Nebit Dag, near the Caspian port of Krasnovodsk, having run from Kerki on the Amu Darya. For its first 375 miles, some distance short of Ashkhabad, the canal is navigable by small freighters, and there is a hydrofoil which rushes up and down near Mary (not far from ancient Merv) for the amusement of tourists. More important though, is the effect of the canal upon the surrounding desert. Along either side of the channel, three million acres of land have been irrigated, and almost half of Turkmenia's considerable cotton crop is the result, together with increasing acreages of fruit, grain, and fodder. Scientists are alarmed by the reduction of the Aral Sea—which has shrunk in volume by 66 percent in the past 29 years—as a result of irrigation's demands upon the Amu Darya. The Turkomans say that the Uzbeks and not they are to blame for this; and the Uzbeks say it is all the Turkomans' fault.

It is hard to think of the Turkmenian capital as an oasis, though technically that is what Ashkhabad is, in the midst of all that arid land. Like the other Central Asian capitals, this is a considerable city and a mostly modern one at that, because its past was virtually destroyed in 1948. But in appearance it is not so different from Kazakhstan's Alma Ata, Kirghizia's Frunze, or Tajikistan's Dushanbe. In each case there are buildings which date back to the 19th century, when the Russian influence was first felt in Central Asia. The roads leading out of each city are often bordered with traditional Russian cottages of wood, painted in pastel or deeper shades, with carved shutters open on either side of the windows. But these are soon overtaken by sometimes depressing varieties of 20th-century architecture, ranging from mass-produced high-rise homes to often grandiose buildings which discharge political, municipal, and cultural functions. There is much space between these and it is usually well planted with trees and shrubbery, except in Tashkent, capital of Uzbekistan and metropolis of the whole region (with a population of two million or so), where there is often space so empty that it becomes oppressive—including, so they boast, the biggest public square in the Soviet Union, dominated by the largest statue of Lenin.

One tends, therefore, to distinguish Central Asian cities from each other less by their appearance than by their surroundings or by some local habit. Alma Ata is thus unforgettably within the clench of mountains that belong to the Tian Shan range, and it has a sumptuous Palace of Baths in which hundreds of naked citizens each day steam, parboil, bake, sluice, and flagellate themselves in a fragrance of birch and pine twigs. Tashkent sprawls tediously, makes aircraft, has a splendid opera house that was considerably less than half full when I saw a production of Tchaikovsky's *Iolanta* there, and a growing new subway system modeled lavishly on Moscow's. Ashkhabad lies close to the dusty ruins of Nisa, ancient Parthia's capital, and among its industries is the manufacture of Turkoman carpets, which three women weave on each handloom, taking a couple of months to produce a work of art that will cover a wall (*much* too fine to be trodden underfoot, according to a factory manager, whose eye was firmly on fastidious and wealthy customers overseas). Tselinograd, which was the administrative center of the Virgin Lands program, now thrives on producing agricultural machinery, and in the steppe's bitter winter constructs for children a magical park of ice. Reindeer, bears, and other beasts glisten amid festooning fairy lights, while the heavily muffled tots ride merry-go-rounds and seesaws late into the evening, as their parents look on.

Semipalatinsk, home for nuclear physicists and high-flying military, claims to have the biggest meat-packing plant outside Chicago, and it certainly has the best stocked food shops I've seen in the Soviet Union or even throughout the Eastern bloc. The queues are shorter than elsewhere, in consequence. What's more, there are restaurants where people treat feeding as a form of dalliance, rather than the often rather grim Soviet business of acquiring nourishment. In Semipalatinsk I have sat in an ice-cream parlor surrounded by young folk who must have been at least partly attracted by the candy-striped walls and the fountain in the middle of the room. They giggled and they flirted with each other exactly as teenagers do in the West.

Samarkand and Bukhara are different, though. Here you feel much closer to the wild and romantic past of Central Asia. Just outside Samarkand is the crumbled residue of Afrasiab, a thriving oasis long before Alexander the Great invaded in 329 B.C. and knew it as Maracanda. Most compelling though, is the legacy of the 14th century and a little later, mostly associated with Tamerlane's supremacy. Flashes of turquoise reveal the glazed tiles on buildings created to his order or to that of his descendants; the Bibi Khanum Mosque, the focus of legends about the misconduct of its architect and Tamerlane's favorite wife; the Gur-i-Emir, the "grave of the king," with Tamerlane's black jade lozenge of a tomb standing beneath the high dome; most lavish of all, the complex of mosques and madrasahs grouped around the Registan ("sandy place" in Uzbek), which the much traveled Lord Curzon, sometime Viceroy of India, thought "the noblest public square in the world." That was in 1888, and it is still a marvel of minarets, domes, archways, portals, and walls, all vividly glazed on the outside and painted brilliantly within. What we see now is a painstaking restoration carried out by the Uzbek architects, and this upsets some purists who prefer their ancient monuments to linger untouched from the past until they collapse into rubble. I sympathize with much of their argument; but even a heavily restored Registan takes my breath away.

In Bukhara the restorers have concentrated on brickwork of the 10th and 12th centuries rather than later tiling. They have helped to preserve a past even more palpable than in Samarkand. Here was the small but almost impregnable fortified oasis in which a succession of mostly unpleasant potentates ruled for centuries until the last emir of Bukhara was extracted by the young Red Army in 1920. Visible for miles beyond the decaying city walls is the Kalyan Minaret, from which criminals—or the merely dissident—were thrown to their deaths. Behind the sloping walls of Bukhara's fortress, in which the emirs dwelt, stands the awful place where their captives were held. It includes the large hole in the ground in which specifically voracious vermin—sheep ticks, scorpions, reptiles, and the like—were maintained so that they would torment prisoners, sometimes for months on end.

Apart from the cruelty practiced there, old Bukhara was notable for one other thing, and that was trade. Marco Polo's father and uncle came here in the 13th century because it was one of the resting places on the fabulous Silk Road between East and West. Anyone traveling today across the southern marches of Soviet Central Asia is generally plodding the line of the Silk Road. Samarkand, as well as Bukhara, was the site of an important caravansary, that ancient forerunner of the motel, where the long-distance travelers could rest awhile and replenish their victuals before pushing on to the next stage in their journey.

Wherever there was a caravansary there would also be a *chaikhana,* a tea shop, and these have survived. Usually there is nowadays an annex with conventional café furniture, and here both men and women may be found. But, in the old fashion, there are always low tables at which travelers and residents, mostly men, sit cross-legged on padded benches while they sip their drinks and slurp their noodle soup and munch hard-boiled eggs. The hard men congregate, the long-distance truck drivers, descended from the muleteers and others who rode in the old caravans, and the local workmen, attracted by birds of passage for the news, and sometimes the bargains they invariably bring.

That traffic along the Silk Road played its part in forming the rich cultural complexity of Central Asia; as, too, did the long history of warfare here, with freebooting armies from every direction forever roaming the steppe and the mountain passes, sometimes settling for winter quarters—often enough coupling haphazardly with the local women. The Tajiks have been in Central Asia longer than any other of its present inhabitants, descended from migrants who moved out of Persia long before Alexander's time. The other chief indigenous groups—the tall and long-headed Turkomans, the shorter and darker Uzbeks, the Kazakhs and the Kirghizes who both bear traces of Mongol blood—came later on waves of migration or conquest.

On any street, in any marketplace, one can see a medley of people whose ancestors settled in at almost any time across a dozen centuries. Near Mary there are Baluchis, whose traditional home straddles Iran and Afghanistan. In Kirghizia, near Osh, there are Dungans, a Chinese Muslim people who fled their native land during the 19th century after religious persecution; and at about the same time the Uygurs also came out of China to make a new home for themselves near Alma Ata. There are Koreans who were resettled from the Far East during some paranoia of Stalin's in the 1930s; and Tatars whom he deported from the Crimea in 1944 as a punishment for collaborating with the Nazis; and Germans who had settled along the Volga during Catherine the Great's time and were shunted into Kazakhstan in 1941 so that they wouldn't be in a position to collaborate.

Among the people now in Central Asia whose origins lie in Europe, a majority are Russians or other Slavs who came in with tsarist expansion and Soviet consolidation. But almost any type of the human race is liable to turn up in these parts. One day in Frunze I watched a thickset man with the mustachioed face of Genghis Khan, wearing a quilted coat and jackboots curled up at the toes, so heavy that he could only walk clumsily in them, like a sailor reeling ashore after weeks at sea. He approached a souvenir stall and thrust a hand into his boot top, where he kept his money. When his visiting delegation had finished its business among the Kirghiz, he would be taking his new trinkets back home to Mongolia.

Beyond the cities, after the last farm village has been left behind in the urban hinterland, the indigenous population dominates the wide open spaces. Almost everywhere except in Tajikistan, whose people have traditionally been cultivators, this means that many spend part of the year on the move with their flocks in search of good grazing across the desert, the steppe, and the mountain pastures. Most of their sheep are bred for both meat and wool, but the Karakul is especially valued for its tightly curled fleece, which Westerners know as astrakhan. I had heard that the most highly esteemed pelts came from lambs cut from the womb a few days before birth was due. Was this true, I asked the director of a Kazakh agricultural institute, and who would want such a thing? Yes, he said with a grimace, it was perfectly true, done to satisfy the vanity of actresses and—he rolled his eyes in despair—"people like that." Then he twinkled conspiratorially. "They're very expensive," he said. "Very expensive indeed—and not very warm!"

And then there is the horse, which was first domesticated in Central Asia 5,000 years ago. There is a stud just outside Ashkhabad where they breed the celebrated Akhal-Teke, which ranks alongside the Arab and the English Thoroughbred as a beast prized by the connoisseur for its speed and stamina. Yet across the length of Kazakhstan, Kirghizia, and Turkmenia there are herds so huge that the stranger wonders what on earth can be the need for them in an economy so long dominated by the tractor. The answer is that they are for the table, slaughtered when they are between two and four years old, dark horseflesh being much more common than beef in any butcher's shop, and more acceptable to his customers. It is, they say, the best meat because it is the cleanest. Unlike the pig and the hen, the argument goes, the horse will eat only grass, and unlike the cow and the sheep it will drink only water that is pure. That may be a rationalization, and no such argument is advanced in support of koumiss, which is a favorite tipple among the people of the steppe. This is fermented mare's milk, sourish in taste, with just a suspicion of bitter bile.

It is during the summer months that these gigantic landscapes become most restless with herdsmen moving their animals slowly across the flatlands and the mountainous slopes. It is then that the Kirghiz shepherds working their flocks along the sides of the Altay range train eagles to hunt small gazelles for the pot. It is then that whole families move from place to place with their dwellings and

161

all their impedimenta; then that the pastures are dappled with the rounded shape of the yurt, the traditional tent of Central Asia, whose panels of thick felt are stretched over a curved frame of willow. Except in emergency, I have seen no one living like this in winter, though I have heard an old-timer in the desert of Turkmenia bemoan the fact that he no longer made his home permanently in a yurt, which was the way he had been brought up, the way he preferred to live. But his family wouldn't hear of it, and insisted on the small but cozy dwelling with concrete walls and a tin roof, which (he grumbled) became too hot, so that you caught cold when you went outside if you didn't look out.

When you see the nomads moving beneath the massive skies of Central Asia, you realize that the most significant boundaries in this part of the world are not political, but natural; mountains most of all. Life was more uneasy than most are yet prepared to admit during the war in Afghanistan, when a lot of their boys who had been conscripted into the Soviet Army found themselves fighting *muja-hidin* who were also Tajiks, or Uzbeks, or Turkomans, or other kinsmen who had been left untidily by history on both sides of the frontier, speaking the same language, heirs to the same culture. The biggest common legacy is Islam, which arrived with Arab invasion at the start of the seventh century.

It is Islam which divides most sharply the indigenous peoples of Soviet Central Asia from the Russians and other Slavs who began to colonize in the middle of the 19th century. The Russians brought their Orthodox Church south (and in Alma Ata every week, the Cathedral of St. Nicholas is packed for the Sunday Liturgy) but in the whole of the Soviet Union there are estimated to be no more than 40 million Orthodox; whereas Kazakhstan and the Central Asian Republics have a Muslim population which is put at 35 million or more. In every market of Central Asia you can see old men selling beads strung onto small garlands which encircle their arms. These are *alfeeya*, which is an Arabic word, and they are not garlands as we understand them but Muslim rosaries.

Every town of any size has its mosque, and Tashkent is said to have 18. The Uzbek capital also houses an Islamic institute where 50 students (including foreigners from South Yemen, Vietnam, Bulgaria, and Afghanistan) are being trained as religious leaders. This is not such an overt form of Islam as is normal outside the Soviet Union; for the amplified call of the muezzin to prayer is not heard here, his natural voice carrying no more than a block or two from the minaret on which he stands in the age-old way. But it is a potent factor in the way most people in Central Asia conduct their lives, in the way they think; and also a powerful link with parts of the world outside.

As are a number of other things. The gorgeous buildings of Samarkand and Bukhara were imitated wherever the writ of the Moguls ran through the Indian subcontinent. The markets of Ashkhabad and Tashkent are much like the bazaars of Peshawar and Lahore, with piles of fruit and vegetables in the open, mounds of spices, dazzling cones of powdered dye, people haggling over prices, weighing things on primitive scales, crying their wares, waiting patiently for someone to buy. On the outskirts of Dushanbe, I have seen patties of cow dung drying on walls before being used as fuel on the cooking fires inside, just as I have seen them down the length of the River Ganges.

But, in Kazakhstan, one echo of a distant land astonished me. In a Soviet version of the jeep, I had embarked with my driver on a long journey under lowering gray skies which gave the undulating steppe, coated with snow, the appearance of a wintry sea; bleak and inhospitable, the sort of place you wouldn't want to break down in. For 120 miles we drove southwest from Semipalatinsk, and in all that emptiness we passed nothing but the occasional truck, saw nothing else but a flock of sheep and a herd of horses, each guarded by a rider who sat motionless in his saddle and stared blankly as we went by. Each was also attended by a pack of ferocious dogs for protection against wolves, and these rushed at the vehicle, snarling with menace. I was glad to be inside it.

e were heading for the village of Karaul which, as its name translates, used to be a settlement of black yurts, but now consists of permanent buildings of concrete, brick, and stone. There's even a little square with the inevitable concrete Lenin on his plinth. It is, nevertheless, a community of purely indigenous people, Kazakhs born and bred. I had been asked to appear as guest of honor at—of all things—a beauty contest for the girls of the village and surrounding district. By the time we got there the village hall was crammed to the rafters, and what looked like a group of traditional musicians was onstage, though just in front a technician was fiddling with sophisticated amplifying equipment.

A score of competitors had reached the finals and they were without exception stunning to behold: dark haired, olive skinned, not quite Caucasian in features, not quite Mongolian, but something ravishingly in between. As each was announced, she glided in from the wings, clad in traditional dress, and began to dance in the traditional way, long skirts swirling, long-sleeved arms flowing, fingers fluttering delicately, head inclined demurely, eyes downcast obediently. It was very Oriental, sweetly chaste, and in every case it was hailed with loud applause. When all had performed their dances, there was a pause. . . . Then the girls reappeared; and they were utterly transformed.

This time each came onstage with her hair down, her hips swiveling, her feet tapping and every other part of her anatomy throbbing to the boom-boom-de-boom of amplified disco noise. Some were clad in leather gear, others in jeans, and a couple of these Kazakh shepherdesses had dared to blouse themselves in see-throughs. All, for the moment, had sent Islam and Central Asia packing. The see-through pair looked as though they'd been studying Travolta videos all winter, and were now imitating meticulously, wildly, suggestively. The noise the audience made throughout was almost as deafening as the music. The applause as each girl finished was ear-aching with wolf whistles. Western decadence had come to this uttermost part of the world with a vengeance. Truly, the conquests of Genghis Khan were as nothing compared with those of Thomas Alva Edison and his successors.

163

Traditional partners of the Central Asian steppe, man and horse now work on state and collective livestock farms, on the expansive grasslands where nomad families roamed centuries ago. This sheepherder makes his home in Kazakhstan—the second largest of the Soviet Socialist Republics. In Kazakhstan and the four republics of Soviet Central Asia—Turkmenia, Uzbekistan, Tajikistan, and Kirghizia—live more than a hundred varied ethnic groups.

This is also a region of geographical diversity. South of the arid Kazakh steppe lie the sun-beaten deserts and lush oases of Turkmenia and Uzbekistan. Extensively irrigated, these lands are deprived of rain by the barrier of snow-clad mountain ranges that stretch across Tajikistan and Kirghizia.

164

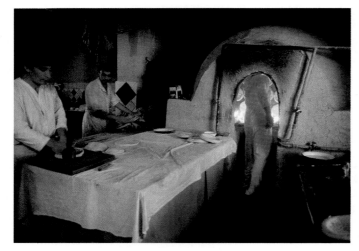

M ounds of melons surround vendors at the bazaar in Samarkand, a Muslim city of 366,000 in Uzbekistan. The short winters and abundant sunshine of Soviet Central Asia provide ideal conditions for melons—hundreds of types grow in Uzbekistan alone—and a multitude of fruit and grain crops.

In the marketplace, women sell naan (above, top), traditional flatbread. At a government bakery in Bukhara, naan is baked every morning in a tandir, a clay furnace fired by charcoal. Secrets of the bread recipes have been handed down through generations.

A small fire on the table keeps the kettles warm for Oounkhan Atayeva as she makes green tea. Seated on carpeted floors in her home in Mary, Turkmenia, family and guests will drink the traditional beverage from bowls. Piping hot green tea keeps its drinkers cool, they claim, and helps them cope with the desert's relentless summer, when temperatures rise to 120°F. A feature of every meal and social occasion, green tea has been enjoyed by Muslims for centuries throughout Central Asia.

Gatherings such as this are typical of large, extended Muslim families. Three or four generations live under one roof, or nearby, so child care is handy and homespun.

169

Ljalja Kuznetsova (also pages 172-173)

To dry their crop in the sun, workers pitch cotton bolls at a state farm in Tajikistan. Cotton rules the economy of Central Asia and ranks the Soviet Union among the world's top three producers. Pressure to keep production high makes this arid region dependent on large-scale irrigation. Thousands of miles of canals drain rivers that once replenished the now endangered Aral Sea.

Near Tashkent, women pick cotton by hand. Machinery harvests about half the crop. Often handpickers follow the machines to glean the fields.

Pages 172-173: Piled sky-high, cotton awaits ginning and baling.

Eggs collected at a poultry plant near Tselinograd, in Kazakhstan, represent an industry that has thrived under Ptitseprom, a special government program. Ptitseprom farms and private households supply most of the chickens and eggs consumed by city dwellers of the USSR.

Geese bring a nice profit to farmers of Ivanovka, a village of ethnic Germans in eastern Kazakhstan. More than 200 years ago, Germans settled along the Volga. During World War II, Stalin accused them of collaboration, and deported millions to Kazakhstan, where they turned the steppe into productive land.

175

P rotected from noxious dust, a worker bags sodium sulfate extracted from Kara Bogaz Gol, a shallow gulf in western Turkmenia. Briny water piped from the nearby Caspian Sea evaporates, leaving deposits of mineral salts. From one of the world's largest sources of sodium sulfate, flatcars convey the salts to factories that make glass, paper, and detergents. Lenin judged Kara Bogaz Gol a bay of treasures—they are treasures hard won indeed from the salty moonscape.

B eneath Lenin's gaze and a slogan extolling the Communist Party as "the leading and guiding force of Soviet society," an Ashkhabad Carpet Factory employee sweeps a new rug. For 700 years women of Turkmenia have woven rugs. Today's carpets, displaying traditional designs and craftsmanship, bring valued foreign currency.

Under a government tolerant of Islam, worshipers depart the Friday service at a Samarkand mosque. Islam persists as a strong cultural force in Kazakhstan and Central Asia. Across the Soviet Union, some 53 million Muslims compose a strengthening political group.

Boys run in the sports complex of the Red October collective farm near Frunze, Kirghizia. The Soviet state promotes sports—recreational and competitive—to make happier and healthier citizens. Showing off their muscles, young wrestlers may dream of competing one day in the Olympics.

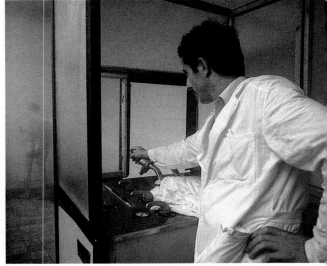

Middle Eastern motifs decorate the anteroom to the women's Oriental sauna at the Palace of Baths in Alma Ata, capital of Kazakhstan. As many as 500 people daily seek out massages here and the 122°F heat of the sauna. For centuries the bathhouse regimen has brought Russians and Central Asians relaxation, preventive treatments, and therapy for a variety of ills. A patron of a resort near the Tajik capital, Dushanbe, receives an invigorating shower of mineral water.

On the frozen Ishim River, a youngster skates before the modern skyline of Tselinograd. Once a dusty Kazakh village called Akmolinsk, this industrial city now supports 277,000 people. In the midst of a region designated for the Virgin and Long Idle Lands program of the 1950s, the developing town was renamed Tselinograd—"virgin lands city"—in 1961.

Pages 186-187: Restored to its original beauty, Registan Square in Samarkand captures the attention of natives, tourists, artists, and officials. The mosaic-covered portals, domes, and minarets of the three madrasahs—Muslim boys' religious schools—typify Islamic architecture of the 15th and 17th centuries. In the 1970s a desire for increased tourism revived restoration work begun in 1921.

185

Sunrise in the Gissar Valley spotlights farmland in the foothills of the Alay Mountains in western Tajikistan. More than 90 percent of the republic is mountainous. The Pamir-Alay range crosses from east to west and includes Pik Kommunizma, the highest peak in the Soviet Union. Mild winters, long, hot summers, and soils irrigated by glacial melt make the valley lush with geraniums grown for oil, cotton, sesame, rice, wheat, and fruits.

189

190

With materials at hand Tajik villagers in the Tian Shan build homes of stone, adobe brick, and sod, often on a wooden frame. Traditionally, houses are built close to each other—not one stands alone—and reflect the tight-knit social organization of Central Asian villages.

Modern-looking structures (opposite, top) in the Alay Mountains' steep Varzob Gorge house a coal-mining camp. Narrow-gauge rail lines and trucks winding down mountain roads transport the fuel to cities.

In Dushanbe, young girls play hand-clapping games in front of a traditional clay house. In this earthquake-prone region, architects are trying to design new buildings to withstand the frequent tremors. But residents of older homes often suffer great losses.

191

A young herder on a bicycle takes camels to pasture in the Kara Kum, the arid heartland covering 80 percent of Turkmenia. Adapted to extreme climates, camels serve as sturdy beasts of burden. Collective farms also breed them for wool, meat, and milk. Because camels can follow rough ter-rain, some sheepherders use them to move their camps as they follow the flocks.

A Tajikistan mountain slope (opposite) provides pasture for Karakul sheep, in the hot, dry climate where this breed thrives. Karakul are especially valued for the skins of their new lambs, born black and curly haired.

A 12th-century Muslim mausoleum stands amid the ruins of the ancient city of Merv, a caravan oasis that grew where the Murgab River forms an inland delta in the Kara Kum. This area has been occupied since the fifth century B.C. In A.D. 646, Arabs conquered the city. Mongols and others followed, all vying for the precious water of the Murgab. When Russians seized the land from Turkomans in 1883, little but ruins remained of the town believed to be the paradise exalted in Arab, Hindu, and Farsi legends.

Today the city of Mary, 19 miles west of the ancient site, supplies Moscow and other faraway cities with natural gas. Cotton farms, orchards, vineyards, and pastureland for cattle and sheep abound on the fertile land surrounding the once great oasis on the old Silk Road.

Siberia & the Pacific Rim

By Douglas H. Chadwick
Photographs by Igor Gavrilov

n south-central Siberia there is a great crack in the Earth. Geologists think it may be because two crustal plates collided to the south, then rebounded. The area still trembles with as many as 2,000 small quakes each year. Mountain ranges 6,000 feet high line both edges. Between them, in the rift itself, floats the oldest of all lakes, so big and clear it is like a second sky. You can pick out a white stone 120 feet deep in its waters, which run more than a mile deep in places and 395 miles long. One of every five drops of fresh water on the planet is in Lake Baykal. So are some 1,500 life-forms found nowhere else, from emerald green sponges to small seals a thousand miles from the sea. Another thing that thrives here is the human spirit.

Not far from where the Angara River flows out of Baykal, I noticed a sailboat named *Rio Grande* bobbing at anchor. It was the handiwork of Yuri Panov, who greeted me at his riverbank house. He had built that, too. All around the wooden structure, and woven into it, were statues carved from driftwood logs. Each had the twisting, haunted quality of a thing freshly dreamed. Lake monsters. Faerie queens and knot-eyed trolls. Wind gods, who move the waters.

"I have been sailing Baykal for 30 years. I have seen 25-foot waves and seen people die in storms. But I love the lake. There is nothing so free as sailing through its beauty. Each piece of driftwood I bring back to carve is a different memory of the wild shores where I go alone to camp and explore." Yuri does not say that he used to sketch cartoons of friends in his army unit during the Stalin era. Or that he was sent to Siberia for it, charged with making anti-Soviet propaganda. Yet upon his release, Yuri Panov stayed on.

Baykal crystallized what many Siberians had been telling me. Their home, infamous as a land of exile and chains, has at the same time offered more raw freedom and fresh opportunities than other parts of the nation. That's what frontiers are all about. And in the immense, resource-laden frontier of Siberia, they said, you will find the future of the Soviet Union.

Europe comes to a halt at the Ural Mountains. On the other side sprawls *Sibir*, the "sleeping land," head resting amidst the barrens of the Arctic, feet touching the steppe of Kazakhstan, Mongolia, and northern China. Historically, everything from the Urals to the Pacific was thought of as Siberia. But now the Pacific rim functions as a separate region. Today's Siberia, then, is roughly the same size as the 50 United States. Although it makes up almost half of the Soviet Union, it contains only 9 percent of the population, or about 25 million peo-

196

Designs from a *nalichnik,* a carved window frame of a house in Irkutsk, Siberia.

ple. However, the region already produces most of the nation's oil, gas, and coal; nearly all its diamonds; and roughly a quarter of its metals and timber, with much more in reserve. Siberia's overwhelming share of the country's fresh water includes not only Baykal but three of the world's largest rivers—the Ob, Yenisey, and Lena, muscling their way north to the Arctic Ocean.

In the republic of Yakutiya, itself the size of India, I glimpsed the way life used to be across so much of the sleeping land. On every side, there was taiga, the northern forest of pine, larch, spruce, birch, and slow, peat-dark streams. Autumn had molted the larch gold and rusted the underbrush. Now, at sunset, one end of the sky took on the same colors. The other end filled with a rising moon, silver as the reindeer moss underfoot. Back toward camp, a man was calling the reindeer, grunting *Hoh! Hoh! Oh! Oh!* From all across the taiga the animals answered and came, trotting in small bands, their coats bark brown and frost white.

The Evenks are one of many native Siberian peoples whose culture revolved around hunting, fishing, and a symbiosis with the domesticated caribou known as reindeer. While those Evenks who continue herding belong to collectives, their techniques have changed little. They keep the animals tame by offering extra food and occasional salt, along with protection from wolves and bears. In summer, they add smudge fires to ward off Siberia's legions of biting insects. "You see," herder Valery Germogenov laughed as we watched the deer file into a smoky corral, "the mosquitoes and gnats are our assistant herders."

The next day we rode reindeer bulls, on saddles of reindeer hide and antler bone, and dined on reindeer meat and marrow. Adding to the table a dish of blueberries in cream from reindeer milk, a woman in her 70s, Ekaterina Aleksandrova, told me, "When we go to the settlements, we stay only two or three days at a time. I don't feel well there, and the children get colds. But here, the air is sweet. We live the strong life. Without the taiga, I could not go on."

This is the richest fur region in the world, and pelts from throughout eastern Siberia and the Far East are shipped to the city of Irkutsk, astride the Angara River 40 miles from Baykal. Here, husks of wolves huddle in bale upon silver bale at the Fur Distribution Center. Ceiling-high heaps of arctic hares and squirrels foreshadow hats. Muskrat pelts lie stacked like so many rubles next to native lynx, foxes, otters. . . .

"Our center also handles 800,000 mink each year and 160,000 sables, the most treasured pelt of all," explained Olga Novikova, who oversees the grading of all this hair. "Of course, many come from fur farms now. But the thickest, warmest fur is always from the wild. I can tell it with a brush of my hand. Workers in the north especially like wolverine trim on their parka hoods, because it sheds the frost that forms from their breath." When I walked out of that multistory mortuary, the afternoon temperature was nearing 90°F. That's not unusual for Siberia in July, especially not for Irkutsk, cradled deep in Asia's interior, and a popular stopover for bright, gold-toothed Gypsy bands and the footloose Siberian hoboes known as *bichi*.

Cossacks founded the city in 1652, and it served as the hub of Russia's steadily expanding eastern domain. In the courtyard of the Znamensky Convent church lie the remains of Grigori Shelikhov, who set up the first European colony along Alaska's coast during the 1780s, and the Russian-American Company. For a brief time, Irkutsk was the religious capital of Alaska. Other churches, a synagogue, and a mosque grace the city and so do stately museums, theaters, and art galleries. The site of Siberia's first institute of higher learning, Irkutsk now has eight. Some 60,000 of its 600,000 inhabitants attend the institutes. "Maybe you thought Siberia was snow and tents?" one student asked while we danced to rock and roll under the stars at a riverside park. "Don't feel bad. Many people in the western part of our own country think the same thing."

Irkutsk was where the iron tracks leading eastward from Moscow and those laid westward from the Pacific port of Vladivostok finally met in 1904, producing the longest railroad on the globe—the Trans-Siberian. Then, after World War II, planners quickly revived a favorite prewar venture; namely BAM, the Baykal-Amur Mainline Railroad. Where the Trans-Siberian turns sharply south at Tayshet, BAM was to branch off and run north of Baykal to the Pacific, opening up 2,000 miles of hinterlands along the way. It was 1984 before this subject of so much glowing propaganda was declared finished. BAM was built partly through the efforts of the Komsomol, or Young Communist League, who came to challenge the elements and themselves. It was also built with army and convict labor, I learned. And to tell the whole truth, BAM isn't done yet.

The first section is functional, anyway, and a city rises where the tracks cross the Angara. Welcome to Bratsk, population 255,000, symbol of the megaproject era. Its three-mile-long dam, completed in 1966, is the second in a series of four that begins in Irkutsk. It has the ninth largest capacity of any hydropower plant in the world. Two more span the Angara before it joins the Yenisey. The world's fourth largest and fifth largest block the Yenisey itself. Plans for bigger ones downstream have been tabled.

The power from this cascade of concrete joins the United Siberian System, which in turn joins the grid for the western USSR. The Bratsk facility was constructed in winter temperatures nearly 60° below zero. But lately, residents say, the thermometer has seldom dropped below minus 45°, and one reason may be the proliferation of such dams. Their huge reservoirs store heat and release humidity, in some places making Siberian winters warmer and summers cloudier.

Recent rains had made life slow for the pilots and smoke jumpers who patrol the taiga for fires. I found them in Bratsk at the Department for the Air Defense of Forests, sharpening shovels and swapping stories. "Each team of six men carries two guns for bears when we parachute in to fight the flames," one told me. "You know," said another, "people used to keep young bears as pets in town and take them to dances." "I had one," added director Anatoly Starodubtsev. "I took it up in a light airplane with me one day so it could see the country. My bear friend became very excited and tangled itself up in the control cables. Well, we had an interesting ride. But now my friend lives in a zoo." "When I first came here, bear was king of the taiga," said a different man. "You could get a bear hunting license if you killed two wolves first. Now there aren't so many wolves, bear is scarce, and moose is the taiga's king."

The taiga's trees feed Bratsk's wood-processing plant, which employs 32,000 and is the largest in the USSR. The nation's largest aluminum smelter is also in Bratsk. Factories help construct Pioneer camps, where workers' children spend summer vacations. Bratsk enterprises also have a ski hill, toboggan run, sailing club, horseback riding facilities, indoor sports clubs, and health resorts.

Yet Bratsk has a health problem so far left untreated. Those colossal assembly line manufactories that are supposed to breathe new life into the sleeping land exhale fluoride, sulfur, and chlorine by the ton. The air stinks and stings. Dead and dying trees ring the city for miles. Fish with angry red splotches float belly up in the Angara. Respiratory problems are widespread. Children have an unusual amount of bone problems, possibly due to excessive fluoride. Is this a workers' paradise lost?

"Bratsk is the crucible of development. What are man's needs? What is really best for him?" Evgeny Urukov, editor of a city paper called the *Red Banner*, asked over evening tea at his apartment. "Fifty percent of our articles now deal with environmental issues. We publish statistics on air and water quality. We name those responsible for pollution. At last, with our help, Bratsk has been given top priority for ecological planning." As I was leaving the Soviet Union, I learned that Evgeny had been fired. But his firing—and the balance of man and nature in Siberia—was the topic of debate in the biggest newspapers in Moscow.

Ust Ilimsk, the end of the road as you follow the Angara north, is so new that one side of an avenue gleams with high-rise apartments while the other is a wall of brooding taiga. It seemed like a techno-colony plopped down on a distant planet. Long-horned beetles helicoptered through the streets by the thousands, two inches from antenna to tail. The steps to the ultramodern shopping center were slippery with their black, crushed bodies. Since one caught in a collar or sleeve might squeeze back with big pincer jaws, proper etiquette in Ust Ilimsk meant slapping these strange taiga sentinels off people's hair and shoulders while you chatted.

In the forest, the beetles were joined by more horseflies, deerflies, biting gnats, and mosquitoes than any planet deserves. Pioneers tried burning birch and using the sap residue for insect repellent, but I could see why they thought winter was the easy time of year. I had come to look at one of the highly mechanized logging operations that supplies Ust Ilimsk's wood-processing plant. The loggers joked that their crews are even more efficient in sub-zero weather, when they have to keep moving to stay warm. But at minus 45°, they shut down the machines; metal parts become brittle, threatening to shatter. As for the human operators, they head off to cross-country ski, ice fish, or try ice sailing on the Ust Ilimsk reservoir. It takes more serious cold to shut down a Siberian.

Half a century ago, western Siberia's Tyumen area exported little but wood.

Roads existed mainly in winter, built of packed snow across the frozen marshland. Mail and other goods traveled by river, then by overland convoys, stopping at post stations for fresh mounts and a meal of *pelmeni*—a sort of ravioli, made in huge batches and stored outside in the freezing air—washed down by a shot of vodka. Then oil was discovered. The farther geologists moved north, the more oil and gas they found. Today hydrocarbons are the USSR's most important export, with Tyumen alone pumping out more oil and gas than Saudi Arabia.

The richest fields were discovered around Nizhnevartovsk. The original inhabitants of the area were the Khanty and Mansi peoples. En route to the place they called Samotlor, or "dead lake," I passed folks fishing and gathering cranberries in the cattail bogs. They walked from place to place, balancing atop the pipelines that carry a million tons of oil out of Tyumen every day.

Workers are attracted to Siberia by wages typically double the national average, which is about 220 rubles per month. Some oil field workers make eight times that. High in a tower overlooking Samotlor, driller Flur Gaynutdinov told me, "We wear head nets for the insects in summer and face masks for the winds in winter. The north is the north, *da?* Before, many people just came for the money and then left after a few years. Now they are finding reasons to stay."

Since 1964, Nizhnevartovsk has gone from a muddy shantytown of 4,000 to a metropolis of 242,000 with a typical Siberian skyline of high-rise clones and construction cranes. "When we bring in more industry now, we try to have the schools and housing and other social elements already in place for the new workers and their families," Ivan Yashchenko insisted as we steamed in a sauna. The former mayor whipped himself with birch branches, turned up the heat, and added, "The north grew us. We owe it something. We are going to make a civilization here, not just raw materials for the rest of the country!"

A quarter of the globe, 47 percent of the Soviet Union, and about two-thirds of Siberia is underlain by permafrost. If you plan to build a civilization in such places, you'd better put it on pilings to let cold air circulate underneath. Otherwise the frozen ground absorbs heat and turns to soup. Take a look at the old section of Yakutiya's capital, Yakutsk, where power poles list at drunken angles above buckled sidewalks and sagging wooden houses. But Yakutsk is also where you'll find help from the Permafrost Institute, which has pioneered designs for northern buildings, pipelines, railroads, and dams.

Yakutiya is definitely the most frostbitten of the world's inhabited regions. A low of minus 98°F was recorded here in the village of Oymyakon. In downtown Yakutsk, the *average* temperature through the "warm" January of 1988 was minus 42°. Mountains to the east and south cut off any warm air masses from the ocean. They cut off moisture at the same time. Central Yakutiya receives less annual precipitation than some deserts. The permafrost layer is 4,750 feet deep in places but because of a lack of snow large areas of eastern Siberia had no Ice Age glaciers. As a result it was an important refuge for animals.

During the Ice Age, Asia was intermittently connected to North America. Most of the New World's large modern mammals, from bison and moose to mountain sheep and bears, originated in Eurasia and came across the Bering land bridge. So did North America's native peoples. From a high bank of the Lena River, I watched the modern cargo ships that supply northern settlements make their way past a Stone Age burial site. Beside me, paleontologist Svetlana Fedoseyeva said, "My husband, Yuri Mochanov, found the first evidence of the Diuktai culture, which appeared in northeastern Asia 40,000 years ago, probably following the mammoths and woolly rhinos along sheltered river valleys. We think they gave rise to North America's Indians. A later, more northern culture, the Sumnagin, migrated in a second wave to become your Eskimos."

South of Baykal, northern forests still claim the mountainsides, but the valleys begin to run wide open with wildflowers and grasses. The silvery shrub that American cowpokes call sagebrush scents the air, and the little wild steppe polecat sometimes sleeps in its shade. The Buryat Autonomous Republic, like Chita to the east and Tuva on the west, was the native land of seminomadic herders with close ties to tribes in Mongolia. Their homes were yurts, surrounded by sheep, horses, and the occasional yak or camel. Buryats make up a third of the republic's current population of about one million, and many now raise sheep, cattle, and hay on collective ranches.

During the 1650s, the Russian Orthodox Church approved a revised liturgy and declared that the sign of the cross should be made with three fingers. A faction called the *Starovery*, or Old Believers, preferred two fingers and the original texts and rites. That opinion got some burned at the stake. Many immolated themselves. Hundreds more were exiled across the Urals. After years of travel, one group came to rest in Buryatia, settling in close-knit farming enclaves.

In the village of Bolshoy Kunaley, Filip Kovalov, age 87, is keeper of the holy books. He and a few elderly companions are all who remain of the *Starovery* here. Settling onto a chair beneath a shelf of antique icons, he folded his big hands and told me, "Young people leave for the cities, and the ones that stay have lost interest in the old ways. Our tradition is to gather on holidays and read from the books. We also read a list of the dead after funerals. Now we have to bring people from other settlements to have enough for a prayer group. Who, then, will read the lists after we are gone? Who will remember and pray for us?"

The first large group banished to Siberia for political reasons were the Decembrists, Russian noblemen involved in an unsuccessful 1825 uprising against the tsar. In 1863, 18,600 members of the Polish intelligentsia who had revolted against Russia's imperial rule found themselves Siberia bound. In both cases the sleeping land was infused with some of the most progressive minds of the day.

Vladimir Lenin was exiled to Krasnoyarsk before the revolution. Joseph Stalin served time near Irkutsk. But once in power, Stalin turned around and banished . . . "we used to say thousands. Now that we are dealing more openly with this part of our history, it looks as though the figure may be millions. How many died, God knows," a Soviet journalist snapped at me with a mixture of anger and embarrassment. "People were starved. Worked to death. Executed. We will find out the whole truth. I am not sure we will ever understand it."

A Buddhist monk named Erdem (Knowledge, in Buryat) Zibikyapov asked me, "If there were no mosquitoes, how would we know pain? If we don't know trouble in life, how shall we know joy?" The golden pagoda roofs of the Ivolginsky temple and monastery rise from irrigated hayfields, where mosquito larvae nourish small fish that may in turn be reincarnated in the stomachs of demoiselle cranes. This is a center of the Lamaist Buddhist movement that arrived from Tibet via Mongolia during the 16th and 17th centuries. Although many Buryats adopted its teachings, others kept their shamanist traditions.

Some 25 miles north of the temple, Buryatia's capital, Ulan Ude, stacks up against the Selenga River. At the Academy of Sciences, scientists are looking into the ancient teachings of Tibetan medicine. Like so many Siberian cities, Ulan Ude is a vigorous jumble of ethnic groups, and they coexist with a remarkable degree of harmony. Buryat and Russian, Yakut and Ukrainian, Evenk and Uzbek work side by side. They govern together. They unite in marriage without discrimination. Siberia began as a remote colony and became synonymous with political intolerance. But, more than ever, this enormous region is being shaped by its citizens, each with an equal share in the future.

Down a dim canyon hung with cobalt sea stars the silver fish beamed like moonlight. At the end, they vanished behind a curtain of seaweed, and I flippered up out of the Sea of Japan onto the Soviet Union's southeasternmost shore. "Oho, and where have you been?" a man was shouting. "Carrying messages to American submarines? Come, spy, and tell us everything." Seven time zones away in Moscow, people were just floundering out of bed. Here by the port of Nakhodka, an autumn afternoon beach party was in full swing. A typhoon had whirled into the festivities earlier, lashing the subtropical hillsides with rain-soaked winds. No one seemed to mind much. Although the air and the ocean seemed equally wet, they also felt equally warm. There was vodka aplenty, and shish kebab sizzled over a sheltered fire tended by Valentin Terekhov.

"It was my very good dream to become a man of the sea, ever since I read *Treasure Island* as a boy," this big, buoyant Russian told me while we ate. For three decades Valentin roved the Pacific and harvested its fish, from New Zealand to the edge of the Arctic ice pack. Now he trains captains and navigators in Nakhodka and arranges outings for sailors on shore leave. Valentin threw his arms wide to frame a Korean swimmer emerging onto the sand, salt water streaming off her hair and into the gale. "A woman coming fresh from the sea," he exulted. "Is there anything more lovely? A goddess! Ah, this is my place!"

Sheltered from the open sea by a collar of steep, green, volcanic hills, Nakhodka is the USSR's chief commercial port on the Pacific. Just 55 miles west lies the main naval port, Vladivostok, whose name means "ruler of the east." Both are part of the Primorye Territory, which borders northeastern China and touches North Korea as well. On the north, Primorye adjoins Khabarovsk. The USSR's biggest island, Sakhalin, and the Kuril Island chain stand offshore. Northward are the Kamchatka Peninsula and the Magadan area where, still farther north, Chukotka stretches to only 53 miles from Alaska. These are the lands of the Pacific rim, a region shaped largely by Valentin's place—the sea.

The spreading floor of the Pacific Ocean, barging into Asia, has crumpled the continent's edge with mountain ranges. Its coastline is part of the Pacific Ring of Fire, studded with volcanic peaks. Kamchatka alone has hundreds; some 20 are still cooking. The peninsula's Kronotskiy Reserve, with its Valley of Geysers, seems a mirror image of Katmai National Park and the Valley of 10,000 Smokes on the Alaska Peninsula. It would even be hard to tell which has the biggest brown bears plunging through willow-edged streams during salmon spawning runs. Mud volcanoes splatter Sakhalin and there are places on the Kurils where you can bathe by digging a hole in hot beach sand and letting it fill with ocean water. Crustal changes spawn earthquakes and tsunamis. All in all, the Soviet Far East stands out as much more rugged than Siberia in topography.

The Far East fishing fleet, the largest and most modern in the USSR, provides 40 percent of the nation's total catch. Artificial beds of shellfish and kelp tended off Primorye's shore mark the beginning of a mariculture industry. And the region's merchant fleet links the Soviet Union ever more closely to the Pacific nations of the most rapidly developing economic region of the globe.

The original inhabitants of these northern latitudes were fur-clad Koryaks and Chukchis, who still maintain some of the largest reindeer herds in the country. In the southern maritime lands dwelled a blend of Tungus tribes from Siberia and native Manchurians. Some wore clothing made of fish skins. Many practiced one of humankind's ancient rituals—the worship and sacrifice of the great bear. In 1649 Yerofei Khabarov and his Cossack troops set off to claim these lands for the tsar and to collect furs from the people along the Amur River.

"Our people believed that the Amur is a dragon," remembered Vladimir Beldy, a Nanai. "When it grows angry it twists, and that is what makes the earth quake. Its water is sacred, and the land and all living things near the river are sacred. My mother would take my hands and row them, so I would learn to be a strong boatman. And she would sing about the beauty of the Amur, about the great fish to be caught. That was the old way." Today Vladimir lives with some 600,000 other Soviets in the city of Khabarovsk, a cultural and industrial center of the Far East. An instructor at the Institute of Sports, he has made a special effort to promote traditional Nanai games: rowing, wrestling, archery, and *chakpan*, which resembles lacrosse played with three-pronged spears.

I hiked through Bolshe-Khekhtsir, a 173-square-mile nature reserve on the outskirts of Khabarovsk, with Vera Kharberger of the Far East Forestry Institute. Vera told me, "Our northern jungle fascinates botanists, because it is where the boreal forest, or taiga, meets subtropical Asia." She pointed out wild apricot, bird cherry, and Amur lilac with wild grapevines climbing up their trunks toward the sun. Among them spread the dark needles of Korean pine and dahurian larch, two favorites of the important Far East timber industry.

In the shade grew a far more valuable export, pound for pound—sold in the United States as Siberian ginseng. Nanai hunters, they say, drank tea made from the herb to improve their endurance, and modern-day Soviets put Siberian ginseng extract in a soft drink called Bodrost, meaning "vigor."

The Soviet Union's main soybean harvests come from the fertile, monsoon-watered lands of the southern Amur. Amur farms play a vital role in feeding northern reaches of the Far East, where few crops flourish. Fiery Kamchatka is an exception. In this subarctic peninsula, people raise vegetables in immense hothouse complexes heated by geothermal energy, and actually export potatoes. Southern Sakhalin Island grows surplus crops, too, and its goods can be sent straight to the mainland by train. The railroad cars are driven onto a giant ferry, floated across to Vanino, and hooked onto the BAM.

BAM and the Trans-Siberian line connect near Khabarovsk, home to the Far East Railroad Institute and its 9,000 students. A candidate in engineering led me down the city's broad central boulevard one balmy afternoon, sampling bookstores and ice-cream parlors. Next to a flower vendor, I noticed a sign on the sidewalk offering Poems For Sale. How much? Armenian Mikhail Petrosov waved his pen and wrote me one for free.

It's not so far from Chukotka to Alaska.
Only one small stream separates us.
Let's build bridges, not burn them down,
For there are no borders to friendship.

When a city official discovered that I had been staying late at night at an apartment where people gathered to discuss politics and philosophy, he was irate. *Who were they!* Well, a lot of students. Some artists. A few rockers, into motorcycles and heavy metal music. *What did they say! Were they critical of anything?*

Yes sir. They thought the Amur was too polluted. They worried about the way our global environment was deteriorating. They weren't sure that governments on either side of the old Iron Curtain were doing enough to remove the possibility of nuclear holocaust. What these young Soviets kept stockpiled by the megaton, though, was hope. We unleashed some together, sang, told terrible jokes, and went on to meet for days afterward around town. If you're so eager for me to leave with good impressions, I told my cranky official, you ought to let me see fewer bureaucrats and more of my new acquaintances. Their idealism, honesty, and easy warmth speak most highly of your country.

Still reflecting upon political tolerance, I boarded the Trans-Siberian and rode a hundred miles west. My destination was Birobidzhan, capital of a district set aside in 1934 as the Jewish Autonomous Region. "Shalom. Welcome to the world's first Jewish state," said Leonid Shkolnik.

Leonid was the editor of *Birobidzhaner Stern,* a Yiddish newspaper printed here and read in 300 Soviet cities and 14 nations. The USSR has 1.8 million Jews, he informed me—the world's third largest Jewish population after the United States and Israel. Under the tsars, Russia's Jews were largely confined to ghettos, and were forbidden to hold government positions. Full citizenship came with the revolution. The idea behind the Jewish Autonomous Region was to give those citizens a place they could call their own, claimed the Communist government, but more probably to funnel colonists into the remote Far East. "In the early years, we must have had 30,000 Jews here," recalled 84-year-old Ilya Blekherman, who was recruited with 50 others from Argentina. "They came from every country. One was an American who put the profits from his Midwest farm into building Birobidzhan. All of us were full of great dreams."

In the village of Waldheim, at what might be called either a Jewish collective farm or a Soviet-style kibbutz, I made my way past herds of dairy cows to the wooden house of Mikhail Mateyashchuk. He tends to the smallest livestock: bees. With its flowerful mix of subtropical plants, the southern Far East is one of the chief honey producing regions of the USSR. Mikhail's beekeeping is a private enterprise—a profitable sideline to his state job as an electrician. "My bees gave me my car and an apartment. These little creatures are incredible workers, and they share everything. So they are clearly communists," he joked, calming the insects with pine smoke so that he could draw a honeycomb from the hive. "Except for the queen, of course. She is a true tsarina."

nd what of the plan for a Jewish homeland? It ran up against disillusionment and the Terror—the tyranny of Stalin, who suppressed religion and ethnic traditions along with political freedom. Synagogues closed; some were torn down. The teaching of Yiddish ended. Seeing that the Jewish Autonomous Region was autonomous in name only, some tried to return to their former homes. Today Birobidzhan's Jewish population numbers only about 12,000.

Yiddish is taught to Russians who take part in Birobidzhan's nationally known Jewish amateur theater. Andrei Permin, an auto factory worker rehearsing onstage with an amateur group, told me, "All of us have had to learn to sing and dance, too. It was very hard. But such expression carries over to your everyday life, and I think that it makes you a little more free. You know, good relaxation is just a change of occupation and of your thoughts. It does not mean being lazy." Ironically, the play was by Isaac Babel, a Russian Jew exiled to Siberia as a victim of Stalin's Terror.

Donning a skullcap, I entered Birobidzhan's only synagogue, a low log cabin. There was no rabbi. Instead, seated on a hard bench with faith shining from every curve of his face, there was 30-year-old Boris Kaufman, a computer operator at a power plant. He bicycles to the tabernacle after work every day—on snow he lets air out of the tires for better traction—to clean the house of worship and to read and pray. Often he is the only one here. "I see fewer and fewer people coming to the tabernacle," his words emerged softly into his long beard. "But I am a religious fanatic, and I refuse to believe my eyes. I am convinced by the holy books that such houses as this will exist until Judgment Day."

Maybe Nakhodka could use a little religion. My first night there, one of the good-time girls trolling for sailors outside the International Seamen's Club had her motorcycle stolen. A few days later, photographer Igor Gavrilov and I joined the wild dance scene at a hotel. Igor left his vest draped over a chair. We returned to find it gone along with the notes and camera lenses in the pockets. We reported the theft to the police. They filled out forms.

Possessions never could be taken for granted in Primorye, where Russia and China jousted for control for two centuries. But after China adopted communism, people and goods moved across its border with the USSR virtually unhindered, and Chinese communities prospered in Primorye and Khabarovsk Territories. Then came China's Cultural Revolution of the sixties. Suddenly, Maoist Red Guards were battling Soviets. Not always with bullets. Far Easterners still talk about the time when, during a lull in the skirmishing, Red Guard troops lined up along a ridgetop, turned their backsides to the Russians below, and, at a signal, all dropped their pants.

A territorial squabble was underway at Nakhodka's open marketplace among piles of Korean melons and the hubbub of fishermen's wives hawking fresh squid and frozen Kamchatka crab. "You injure me! You are stealing my sales!" Aleksandr Vinnichenko, age 70, was shouting. And he kept shouting until the woman who had tried to crowd her wares into his stall space moved, leaving Aleksandr and his garden-fresh eggplants in firm control of the countertop. "My grandfather was exiled here in 1904 for bolshevism, and my father lived through the Civil War years when the Far East was the last stronghold for the White Army," he told me. "Americans came here to support them when I was very young. You are one of the first I have seen since then."

Nevertheless, since 1978 Nakhodka has been the Soviet headquarters for a joint venture with U. S. fishermen. Anatoly Kolesnichenko, Director of the Active Marine Fishery Base, explained. "Your trawlers bring their catch to our big mother boats on the open sea. We process the fish and take it in smaller boats to our ports, sell it, then split the profits with the Americans." Soviets also send fish to the U. S. in return for prefabricated building material to help ease the Far East's severe housing shortage.

At the edge of Nakhodka Bay I worked briefly on a crew transferring pipes from Japanese ships onto railroad cars bound for the interior. While great cranes swung fresh bundles overhead past the sun, we cinched down earlier loads with cables. Pausing to mop sweat from the headbands of our hard hats, we traded camping and hiking tales, and compared the prices of cold beer in our two countries, shouting the whole time above the screech of moving metal.

Down the dock at the Far East Steamship Company, welders were mending the ice-beaten prow of a freighter that hauled timber from the mouth of the Yenisey River across the Arctic Ocean to Japan, then returned laden with U. S.

and Canadian grain. Other machinists were racing against the coming of winter to repair an icebreaker for Magadan.

The Sea of Okhotsk, off Magadan, is the nation's richest single source of fish. Magadan itself was first developed for goldfields, also the nation's richest, where political prisoners mined the ore under arctic conditions along the Kolyma River. Only Siberia can match the Far East's combined mineral resources, from gold, tin, and titanium to coal, gas, and oil, including enormous offshore fields now being developed near Sakhalin. For all its natural wealth, which includes a quarter of the USSR's timber reserves, the Far East economy has grown more slowly than that of the country as a whole. The region and its needs have simply proved too remote for the highly centralized Soviet government to deal with effectively. In the future, officials remarked, the Far East must look less toward distant Moscow than out across the ocean that so many nations share.

Nakhodka's busy new eastern port complex, Vostochnyy, has just such a view. It was built to handle coal brought primarily from Siberian fields via BAM. During winter, eight to ten railcars and their hard frozen cargo can be driven at one time into a special building that a technician proudly described to me as a sauna for trains. After the cars are heated, machines turn them upside down like toys to empty their loads. Conveyers funnel the coal into ships' holds at the rate of 3,000 tons per hour, 1,240,000 tons per year, destined primarily for Japan. From Japan comes a variety of electronic equipment and factory technology. Plus nearly 50,000 tourists annually. Most arrive on the ferry from Yokohama, then board the Trans-Siberian for cities open to foreign visitors.

I saw Japanese goods on their way to France and French products headed for Japan. The docks also held rows of Soviet automobiles for shipment to China. Plans call for opening navigation up the Amur to China and for regular air service between Khabarovsk and the Chinese city of Harbin. For that matter, there is talk of a commercial air route between the Far East and Alaska.

If even a fraction of the proposed joint ventures with various nations of differing political views that I heard about come to pass, the Soviet Union will have raised the interdependency of the world's peoples to a new pitch. Such activity might start the Far East on its way to becoming the most dynamic part of the country. It also bodes well for an idea that my student friends in Khabarovsk so often spoke of: Peace on Earth.

From a tower overlooking Nakhodka's ports and the green volcanic hills that enfold them, Viktor Federov keeps track of ship traffic. Or, rather, stacks of Japanese and American computer equipment linked to radar dishes keep track for him, displaying the speed and course of each vessel in the harbor. There were 3,000 in 1987. From Singapore, Cuba, Greece, Poland, Panama. . . . "Sometimes, the quiet water close to shore freezes over," Viktor said. "But I can tell you exactly how thick the ice is on any day." What kind of device in this high-tech navigational center can do that? He replied, "I go out on my lunch break and drill holes through the ice to catch fish. Fishing! It is my craziness. One day you must stay and catch some with me." I see no reason why I couldn't.

207

Galen Rowell, Mountain Light

In May the last of winter's ice floats like clouds on the crystal waters of Lake Baykal, arcing 395 miles through the taiga of southern Siberia. Though more than 300 rivers and mountain streams feed the mile-deep lake, Earth's deepest, only the Angara flows out. In Baykal's depths live some 1,500 unique plant and animal species that evolved over the lake's 25-million-year history. The translucent golomyanka, an oily fish, feeds at the surface at night but may plunge thousands of feet into abyssal darkness by day. A tiny crustacean, the epishura, helps keep the water pure, so that light penetrates the frozen surface to sustain microflora. Like the world hidden beneath the water's surface, Baykal itself is one of the treasures of Siberia, whose great, cold surface belies an abundance of resources and tenacious life.

John deVisser, Black Star

P elts by the thousands are sorted in the fur center at Irkutsk. Some of the best will turn into precious hard currency at the Leningrad fur auction, where foreign buyers bid for the world's most luxurious furs.

In Yakutiya, members of the Yakut Writers Union strike out for rabbits in the season's first snow, following the footsteps of fur trappers and traders who led the Russian charge across Siberia in pursuit of the sable, prized for its thick and lustrous coat. Now state farms and collectives raise many of the animals, but hunters and trappers still scour the taiga.

211

Seny Norasingh. Fred Mayer, Magnum (opposite)

Like flowers snipped from a garden, whole trees are felled and piled by the mechanical arms of the Soviet wood industry. Stripped trees may be sliced into lumber or left as round-wood logs (right), in which the USSR leads world production. Others, chopped into chips, feed immense cellulose factories like this one at Ust Ilimsk, where the wood products complex is designed to chew through millions of cubic feet of wood a year. The Soviet Union sweeps across millions of acres of forested land, two-thirds of it in Siberia and the Far East.

212

All wood and snow, the coal mining settlement of Chulman in Yakutiya seems a relic from pioneer days. And it is, in a way. Formerly the regional mining center, Chulman has been surpassed since more accessible coalfields were found 25 miles away, where the city of Neryungri sprang up in the early 1970s. One of Siberia's new breed of mining centers, Neryungri and its satellites have a population of 100,000; highrise buildings; sophisticated machinery; and a spur of BAM, the Baykal-Amur Mainline Railroad.

215

Stan Grossfeld, Boston Globe

Yevgeny Yevtushenko

n laboratories beneath the world's coldest inhabited region, scientists at the Permafrost Institute in Yakutsk study permanently frozen ground and provide advice to northern industries. Raising buildings and pipelines up on pilings is one method used to avoid melting the permafrost, which may lead to collapsed or sunken structures. Summer thaws also bring problems when the soil above the frozen subsurface turns into a morass of mud.

In the land of "eternal frost," as permafrost is known in parts of the north, gravediggers must fortify themselves for long hours of thawing the earth before digging.

217

orches of waste gas shoot out jets of fire above the ice of western Siberia at Samotlor, the largest oil field in the USSR. Samotlor opened up during the expansion of Soviet oil production that quadrupled national output between 1960 and 1985. Samotlor now pumps nearly 100 million tons of oil annually from more than 5,500 wells. Rapacious development brings abundant oil today, but wells have begun to slow. At the current rate of extraction, even this huge reservoir will have a short life.

Steve Raymer, National Geographic Staff

T he watchful gaze of Lenin follows citizens out for an October stroll in Ulan Ude, capital of Buryatia (above). In Irkutsk (opposite), shoppers throng the damp pavement of Uritskiy Street in the center of town. A 17th-century Cossack encampment, now a city of half a million, Irkutsk is a cosmopolitan center of southern Siberia.

Far to the east, men of Birobidzhan concentrate on a game of dominoes in the capital city of the Jewish Autonomous Region.

R uffles and polka dots give a lift to the Far East clothing industry at a fitting at Khabarovsk's House of Models. A taste of glasnost's new sense of style, however, can't change the cold facts of life in this area. The Birobidzhan mill, spinning out millions of warm socks each year, will likely be around long after miniskirts à la russe have become passé.

Pages 224-225: At a Russian-Buryat wool cooperative near Ulan Ude, a worker marks sheep with blue paint.

Seny Norasingh

223

S affron robes, golden pagoda roofs, and Buddhist services (above) at the Ivolginsky Datsan tell of centuries of Mongolian and Tibetan influence in Buryatia. The datsan is one of a few Buddhist monasteries left in the USSR. Dozens of monasteries once served the nomadic pastoralist Buryats, but repression in the 1930s left only several hundred lamas where there had been thousands. The traditional shamanist beliefs of some Buryats include sacrifice to spirits of the dead, and offerings such as coins, bright berries, and fermented mare's milk at springs, mountain passes, and other places of natural power.

227

Cars of the Trans-Siberian Railroad speed through the taiga near Irkutsk. From here the tracks stretch some 3,000 miles west to Moscow and 2,500 east to the port of Vladivostok. Siberia's famous line will soon share more of its heavy traffic load with BAM, which starts at Tayshet, runs north of Lake Baykal, and will reach the Pacific upon completion. Building the BAM (above), with its 2,000 miles of track, 3,000 bridges (many over a half mile long), and 9 major tunnels has been an arduous and expensive task. Some trains run on the first section (right), but it may be years before Siberia's resources can ride the length of BAM.

Fred Mayer, Magnum

The forbidding Siberia of Western imagination comes to life where one of the Indigirka River's many tributaries snakes through the Moma Range between Yakutsk and the valley of the Kolyma River. Masses of ice cling to sparsely forested valleys in the sandstone and siltstone mountains. Higher up on the peaks, which rise some 7,000 feet, only tundra vegetation can survive. In the Kolyma basin lay the labor camps of the infamous Gulag system, where political prisoners labored with picks and shovels to wrest gold from the frozen ground.

P orts of the Soviet Far
East are vital supply
links for people of the
north and gates to trade with
neighbors such as Japan. But
the main spur to coastal development has been military.
Vladivostok (right), a busy
commercial harbor, has also
played a major role in the massive naval buildup in the

Pacific since World War II.
Soviet seamen are a com-
mon sight in Nakhodka, where
sailors based there number
more than a third of the population. Nakhodka now sees
both foreign trade ships and
those of the huge Soviet merchant fleet. Some Soviet ships,
designed to do double duty, are
convertible for military use.

232

I n Tolbachik's most violent eruption in history, the volcano shook Kamchatka in 1975, spewing lava and billowing ash and steam into the air over the peninsula, part of the Pacific Ring of Fire. On quiet days, tourists enjoy autumn colors at the Kronotskiy Nature Reserve (above), which protects more than 3,500 square miles of lava plateaus, volcanic cones, geysers, and hot springs, as well as Kamchatka's brown bears, foxes, wolverines, lynx, and sables. Active tectonically and economically, the Pacific rim of the Soviet Union is no longer "the end of the world" that it was to Russian schoolchildren of old.

The Arctic

By Yuri Rytkheu
Photographs by Vladimir Vyatkin

true Northerner never embarks on a journey in the polar night. Traditionally he begins his long sleigh ride when the sun has just begun to ascend above the horizon, its rays cool, the traveler's shadow long, and the snow crust still strong.

In February I began my journey through the Soviet Arctic, which stretches from the shores of the Bering Strait to the old Russian city of Arkhangelsk and the port of Murmansk. My route passed through lands populated by the indigenous Northerners who mastered these rigorous places long before the arrival of the Russians. Approximately twenty ethnic groups live here, officially called "small peoples of the North" although their territory constitutes almost one-half of the USSR.

My starting point was Mys Dezhneva, on American maps, East Cape. It also has its own age-old name in my native language, Chukchi: Peek.

This is Chukotka, the northeast extremity of the Eurasian continent, and it is where I was born, in the village of Uelen. Beyond lies another hemisphere, another continent: North America. The cape is a stone ledge, overgrown with moss. Strong winds have polished the stone so that new snow will cling only until the next wind. Winter has two hues: black and white, stone and snow. It seems that no power can change these colors, yet the sun does. In the early morning its rays paint the snow in rosy tones that enliven the dark, gloomy cliffs.

Ivan Segutegin, a resident of Uelen, has watched this scene over some 50 years. From the height of a rocky ledge he easily distinguishes Big Diomede and Little Diomede Islands, almost fused on the icy expanse of the Bering Strait. Big Diomede, or Ratmanov, belongs to the Soviet Union, and Little Diomede to the United States. The distance between them is about two miles, the real distance between two great powers. For the Chukchis and Eskimos, hunters of the whale, walrus, and seal, the strait was the source of life.

Ivan Segutegin returns from hunting. Long before daybreak, when the scarlet bands of dawn had just appeared over the ice, he had risen, breakfasted, and dressed, as his sea-hunter ancestors had dressed for centuries, in seal fur *torbaza* (native boots) and a fur *kukhlyanka* (shirt). On top he wore a white cloth parka. His equipment, not counting his carbine with its telescopic sight, is of the old style: a thin strap, a pointed staff for testing ice strength, and a wooden spear studded with sharp hooks for pulling his catch from the water.

Segutegin walked under the shore cliffs to step out onto the drifting ice. He was seeking an expanse of open water where he would lie in wait, on the edge of

Seal bone carving in the style of the Arkhangelsk region.

the floe, for leaping ringed seals.

Today's hunt was successful. The strap holds a fat ringed seal. As the sun's low rays struck the white snow and piled ice hummocks, Segutegin was already on the way home; his long shadow preceded him on his hunting path.

Segutegin could have ridden to hunt on his snowmobile or his dogsled. Yet he is not only a hunter, but an award-winning artist, a well-known walrus tusk carver. He told me that it is during his unhurried hunting that the images he embodies in his work come to him. He walks slowly along the shore, choosing his path among ice fragments, holding his course to Uelen, where, although born in a hut of walrus skins and reindeer hides, he has lived for some time now in a house with central heating, television, and a telephone.

The main theme of Ivan Segutegin's work is the traditional life of his people, the Chukchis, who today number about 14,000. Most live in Chukotka with 1,500 Eskimos. Approaching the snow-covered Uelen spit, Segutegin came across Yakov Tagyek, a native of the now abandoned Eskimo village of Naukan, on Mys Dezhneva. Both hunters walk silently for a while, then the usual conversation about ice conditions, currents, and weather takes place. Tagyek has had luck too. He also drags a ringed seal. The sun rises, lighting the hunting path and the houses stretching along the spit in two even rows.

The hunters split up beyond a ridge of ice hummocks. Ivan Segutegin walks up to his house, where his wife awaits him at the threshold with a dipper of cold water. The hunter pours some water over the muzzle of the dead seal, drinks the remainder himself, and only after this ceremony brings his catch into the warm room to skin and dress with his broad knife.

I asked Ivan Segutegin about this "watering the seal." He smiled and answered: "I've always performed this ceremony. It kindles interest in life and adds taste to it, and evokes respect for all living things."

Just as the seaside inhabitant of Chukotka has always depended on the hunting of marine animals, his tundra brother has always depended on the reindeer. As I stand by the Kurupkan River, southwest of Uelen, the sun's rays light a patch of shrubbery on the bank. The shrubbery suddenly divides and begins to move. Only now can I see that this is a large herd of reindeer. Herdsman Vladimir Tutay is dressed for winter: fur pants, *torbaza* lined with moisture-absorbent tundra grass, and a *kukhlyanka*. On his head Tutay has a light hat with earmuffs and a cut-out crown; the head never sweats in such a hat.

Tutay tends his reindeer on a hilly plain. There is no forest here, only tall shrubs on the riverbanks. Toward the seacoast are high hills, then rocky precipices. February temperatures reach minus 40°F and lower, with gale-force winds. The 2,000-head herd belongs to the sovkhoz, but Tutay's ancestors have herded reindeer from time immemorial and in the depths of his soul this herdsman considers these his own.

Tutay's tundra dwelling, or *yaranga*, stands on an elevation. The exterior of his cylindrical home is part tarpaulin, part reindeer suede stretched over wooden poles that meet to form a cone-shaped roof. Until recently, a *yaranga* was fashioned entirely of hides. One enters the warm inner room through the cold outer part; through the smoke of a fire I see a wireless radio, a heap of old magazines, and the bed curtains sewn from select, fleecy reindeer hides. As we await a nourishing supper, we listen to the fresh morning news from Moscow, ten time zones away.

South of my itinerary live the Koryaks and Evens. The Koryaks populate the northern part of the Kamchatka Peninsula; some scholars believe it was there that the Chukchis adopted reindeer herding from them. There are about half as many Koryaks (7,900 according to the latest available census) as Chukchis, and the two peoples are close in language and way of life. In addition, the Koryaks are skillful fishermen. Enormous schools of salmon spawn in the rivers of the Kamchatka Peninsula and until recently there were fish enough for humans and for winter feed for dogs as well. In my childhood, feeding dogs meant the same as eating for myself; we ate from the same chunk of frozen walrus meat lopped off with my ax.

My next stop was near the mouth of the Kolyma, one of the largest rivers of northeast Asia, at the rapidly developing settlement of Cherskiy. Freight for eastern Yakutiya, Magadan, and Chukotka is processed here. Ships equipped for sailing among ice floes alone or escorted by icebreakers call here from the west and from the east.

Ten years ago, the last time I was in Cherskiy, empty land stood between the settlement and the port. Now I was returning with my old friend Nikolai Tavrat, for many years chairman of the local soviet. I did not realize that we were approaching the port because new houses covered the once vacant land. Nikolai Tavrat is a Chukchi, and a born polyglot, jumping in conversation from his native language to Russian to Yakut to Yukaghir.

The northern branch of the Yukaghirs live in the Cherskiy area. Several centuries ago, the Yukaghirs were the most widespread indigenous population of the northeast coast of the Arctic Ocean. There remain today only 800 individuals. This minuscule group stubbornly retains its place on the land and shows every tendency toward expansion. Recently, Yukaghir linguist and poet Uluro Ado compiled and published the first Yukaghir primer.

Here, in March, the snow still lies indestructible. I looked at the hotel thermometer: morning temperature, minus 49°F. Yet many fishermen work without gloves. From their nets they pull quivering fish—broad whitefish, white salmon—and the spray freezes in midair; the fish move for only a few minutes. I was amazed that the fishermen could work in such cold with their bare hands.

"The water is warm," explained one of the fishermen. "Compared with the cold air, you can warm yourself in the Kolyma water. It's above freezing."

To the south live the Evens, the "reindeer riders." On their small but sturdy reindeer they cover enormous distances of the forest-tundra. Evens live in western Chukotka, on the Arctic coast, and on the shore of the Sea of Okhotsk, and altogether number 12,500. They populate the transition zone between tundra and taiga, often choosing the most inaccessible locations. Thus, in 1958, in the Rassokha River basin near the Kolyma, I visited a group of nomadic Evens who were unknown to the local authorities and who were unaware that there had been a revolution in Russia, and that they were Soviet citizens.

Thirty years ago these Evens lived in the domain of the powerful Gulag system, which worked the gold mines of the Kolyma using a labor force of political prisoners and a few criminals. Vestiges of the camps can still be seen here and there on the riverbanks: rusted barbed wire, rickety or collapsed watchtowers, remnants of cemeteries, where over the nameless graves stand only stakes with tin can bottoms hammered to them, etched with the unfortunates' identification numbers and the numbers of the articles under which they were convicted.

Beyond the Kolyma is the Yakut land. Spring is impetuous in Yakutiya. As it arrives from the south it drives the ice breakup of the great Lena River into the Arctic Ocean. If I had been traveling by dogsled, I would now have no more path. The sun had devoured my sleigh road, and the rivers barred my way with their high water.

Yakutiya has succeeded in conserving its traditional economy, including its place as the northernmost area for dairy cow breeding as well as horse breeding for meat and milk for koumiss, a wonderful restorative beverage. And of course, reindeer herding.

In all the reindeer herding centers, beginning on the Chukchi Peninsula and ending on the Kola Peninsula far to the west, at approximately the same time, a "harvest" is taking place; the "crop" was raised under the polar night, in wintry gales. In the rare quiet hours beneath the flashes of the northern lights, the reindeer are calving on the thawed patches; fuzzy little fawns appear.

Reindeer number about 2,500,000 throughout the Soviet Union. The history, art, song, dance, clothing, food, and drink of the true Northerner are all connected with the reindeer. Even the cosmology of the people of the tundra and taiga was linked with this animal. When in my childhood I learned the structure of the starry sky, I was taught that the movement of heavenly bodies was the movement of reindeer around the Driven Stake—the North Star.

For the people of the North, the preservation of reindeer is the preservation of their uniqueness. Yet industrial development is striking its most painful blow precisely at reindeer herding. Once the wonderful, voluminous Ichuveyem River flowed into Chaun Bay of the Arctic Ocean. I spent many fine days of my youth on its banks. But when last year, after 20 years' absence, I came back, I could not find the river at all. It had ceased to exist. Dredging for gold had consumed it. The terraces had been stamped out and fertile reindeer pasture destroyed by tractor treads and heavy construction equipment.

I don't know how much gold was gained by this dredging operation. But even tons of riches cannot re-create a single fish that had lived in this river, not even a tiny one, let alone the fish fit for a tsar—white salmon, broad whitefish, muksun, and Arctic cisco.

Even though ice still clings to the shores, Dudinka and the other Arctic ports are already prepared for navigation. The Northern Sea Route stretches some 4,000 miles through the Arctic Ocean, from the Barents Sea to the Bering. It was explored and used commercially as long ago as the 16th century, but after the Russian Revolution it became a regular main line of transportation. Today it is serviced by powerful icebreakers, including several that are atomic powered. Northern sailors dream of turning this sea route into a year-round highway.

The sun rises higher, bringing to the tundra and forest-tundra a short but wonderful season: summer. The nights become shorter. On the polar islands, the sun no longer dips below the horizon at all. Everything hastens to live.

The tundra in summer bloom seems like a natural carpet. The opinion exists that Arctic flowers have no scent, but this is not true. On a quiet, sunny day toward the end of summer, the tundra is permeated by the most varied aromas, enough to give the uninitiated a headache. The tundra berries pour out their juice. Among them the cloudberry, queen of the tundra, glows red. There are mushrooms in abundance. Mushrooms are the reindeer's favorite delicacy, in this season preferred above all other plants, even their winter staple, reindeer moss. The young animals that appeared in the snowy spring are growing. It is now in early autumn that the calves' skin attains its best condition. The fur is resilient and thick, perfect for good winter clothing.

The sun is still high. Sometimes such hot days come to the Arctic that people venture out to swim in a tundra lake. However, even if the water's surface warms up, the swimmer's feet will sense the unmelting ice at the bottom.

The hubbub of a new crop of migratory birds fills the air. They try their young wings in order to set out soon on their journey far across the tundra, the Siberian taiga, the Central Asian deserts, and the high mountain ranges to Africa, Southeast Asia, and other places with warm, easy winters. Only ravens, ptarmigan, and snowy owls stay here in the Arctic tundra.

T he Northern summer is short. Snow can fall as early as August. So I continued my journey following the sun. Ahead was Taymyr—the northernmost projection of the continent. At the tip of Taymyr is Mys Chelyuskin, at 77°43' north latitude. A rich river system laces the peninsula. Foremost among its waterways is the Yenisey, more than 2,000 miles long and navigable 400 miles upriver for maritime vessels.

In Norilsk winter had already arrived. A wind swept the Alykel airport, and snow lay all about. In the overflowing terminal I found the poet Ogdo Aksyonova waiting for me. She drove us on a dirt road to Dudinka, a port near the mouth of the Yenisey. We left behind us Norilsk, founded in 1935, by a special resolution of the government, to be a center of mining and metallurgy. Norilsk has endured a great deal in its history, including the Stalinist period of prisoners' and exiles' forced labor.

Darkness has long since fallen. A typical tundra landscape rushes past the car windows: low shrubs along the river bottoms, freshly snow-powdered hummocks. Now and then a souslik, or ground squirrel, appears in the headlight beam, standing stiff. From time to time in the darkness we hear the echoing clatter of wheels parallel to our road: freight cars rolling on the tracks from Norilsk to Dudinka. The snowfall intensifies and abates by turns, and then the glow of the big city appears dead ahead.

The next morning, regardless of the heavy snowfall, I visited the city, with its many multistoried concrete buildings. The main square is directly above the port with its cranes, warehouses, and rows of containers ready to ship. Dmitri Dudinkov, Deputy Chairman of the soviet, received me in the office of a grandiose building and spoke enthusiastically of Dudinka and Taymyr. The Taymyr Autonomous District occupies almost 350,000 square miles, and, excluding the 175,000 people of Norilsk, has a population of 55,000. The chief pursuits of the indigenous people are reindeer herding, hunting, and fishing.

On a rare fine morning we managed to get away by helicopter to Lake Taymyr, the Arctic's largest body of fresh water. The average depth is about 19 feet, although in some places it is as deep as 80 feet. Six rivers flow into the lake, with only one flowing out—the Lower Taymyr. Usually animated in summer, today Lake Taymyr seemed lifeless, and only here and there could I hear the screech of a lone bird on the wing. We wanted to see the snow sheep in the Putorana hills nearby but we were to be disappointed. Clouds moved in, snow began to fall, and we returned quickly to Dudinka.

I tumbled wet and shivering into Aksyonova's cozy apartment. She had Siberian ravioli—*pelmeni*—and strong tea all ready even though she had spent the day working. Ogdo Aksyonova is a Dolgan. The Dolgans, whose population is about 5,000, are a people related to the Yakuts. Aksyonova is compiling a dictionary of her native tongue and will soon publish a textbook of Dolgan grammar.

"It is our wish that the sound of our language not disappear as long as the Dolgans themselves are alive," states Aksyonova. "Even in the bleakest years, when there was talk all around about how useless and dead-end our languages are, about the backwardness of our cultures, we had radio broadcasts in our native language. People listened in from the Taymyr tundra's most remote outposts. My real dream, though, is to establish writing in my native language.

"I was born in the Avam River tundra, in the nomad camp Volochanka, and for me, the life of the reindeer herder, with its perpetual wandering, was as natural as breathing. I pitied people tethered, like a mean dog, to one and the same place. Day in and day out, they see the same old landscape, the same old horizon, they drink water from only one single source, and don't know how different water tastes from different streams and rivers, different lakes, and the surface of the ice. Even after I started boarding school, I was so drawn to the tundra that I ran away to my parents when they were near Volochanka with their reindeer, and the teachers would catch me, and send me back to the school."

After high school graduation, Aksyonova worked in a propaganda tent, a mobile unit which included a teacher, a film projectionist, a lecturer, and a doctor. Amateur performers sometimes joined them. They followed the nomads. On quiet evenings, when the weary herdsmen returned to the tents, Aksyonova recited poetry in their native Dolgan. The old men listened to the sounds of their language with pleasure and the young people with a sense of unexpected discovery of the beauty of their language.

Ogdo Aksyonova published her first anthology of poetry in 1974, a dual language edition in Dolgan and Russian. Thanks to her efforts, Dolgan is now taught in the early grades of many Taymyr schools. Aksyonova spends several months of every year in the tundra among the hunters and herdsmen. In winter she chooses a time to go out on the ice of the mighty Yenisey to compose poetry in peace and silence among the fishermen. Many of her compositions are sung in far-flung Dolgan villages, schools, and nomad tents.

I have loved Taymyr from my early years,
Covered with a tundra carpet,
Here is my native land, my world,
My snows, my warm home.

I left Dudinka on a dark, wintry dawn. My traveling companion, the sun, rose as the airplane set its course for the west. On Novaya Zemlya and the other Arctic islands far to the north, the polar night was already descending. Ahead of me, I could see columns of smoke for many miles around, not the smoke of herdsmen's tents, but gas torches burning with a sinister yellow flame.

These are the famous deposits which were discovered on the lands of the Nenets, Khanty, and Mansi peoples. Among the nationalities of the North, the Nenets have a fairly large population of 35,000. They have herded reindeer, hunted, and fished since time immemorial. The Nenets were probably the first among all the Northern nationalities to encounter the Russians, in the 16th century. The Nenets accepted baptism and paid tribute—the *yasak*—to the Russian tsar. The *yasak* was subsequently levied on almost all of the peoples of Russia's North up to the revolution, creating the marvelous image of the Russian ruler as someone perpetually suffering from the cold and in need of enormous quantities of soft, warm furs.

Somewhat to the south of the Nenets live the Khanty and Mansi nationalities, whose roots go back to a kinship with the Hungarians. These small groups (the Mansi people, 7,500, and the Khanty, 21,000) are northern branches of the once powerful and numerous Finno-Ugric tribes, who later settled eastern Europe in the territory of modern Hungary, Finland, and Estonia.

It is these regions which are now the main source of oil and gas for the European part of the Soviet Union, although new deposits are being developed on the continental shelf in the Arctic Ocean. The tempo of drilling in the Yamal-Nenets and Khanty-Mansi areas was rapid. In the 15 years from 1965 to 1980, the yield rose from one million tons of oil to over 300 million.

The euphoria of the early years, however, has been displaced by concern. Development of oil and gas deposits has had ruinous effects on the environment. In the last few years alone, five sovkhozes of the Yamal-Nenets area situated in a railroad construction zone have lost almost 1.5 million acres of grazing land and 24,000 reindeer. In their native dwelling places, the smaller national groups of the North are becoming barely noticeable minorities amidst the population of newcomers, chiefly concerned with earning lots of money.

Most cities of the Arctic, especially the new ones, are clones of each other. Even the main streets and squares have the same names. But I had to stop in the old Russian city of Arkhangelsk, which dates its history back to 1584 and played a notable role in the development of the Russian North. Arkhangelsk stands on the bank of the Severnaya Dvina River, which flows into the White Sea. It is a major port with a population of 416,000. Despite the abundance of lumber and chemical industries, Arkhangelsk is a seafaring city. Here live the descendants of those who went "to meet the sun," far to the east, in search of "the fish tooth" and "the soft junk," as walrus tusks and fur were called in earlier times.

he Arctic Circle's proximity is evident. At 5:00 p.m. it is dark. I was met at the airport by Andrei Miller, a man of the seacoast. Andrei has sailed on these waters his entire life. Treating me to fresh-salted white salmon and vodka, he took from a cupboard the family tree he had compiled and decorated with his own hand. Among his relatives I saw not only Russians, but Nenets.

"Where did you get a name like Miller?" I ask my host.

"Sometime around 1854, it seems, a German slipped into our seacoast family," replies Andrei Aleksandrovich. "After all, was there anybody who didn't sail, or earn a living from seals, walruses, or fur! The Russians from Novgorod, the Scandinavians, Norwegians, Swedes, and the Germans, the Dutch . . . ."

Andrei Aleksandrovich was born on Novaya Zemlya. His father hunted for seal and walrus in the summer and set traps for arctic fox in the winter. Life was harsh and often hungry, but free. Love towards his native land remains in Andrei Aleksandrovich's heart. Later, after becoming a sailor, he frequently returned there, bringing supplies to the fishing and hunting cooperatives. Andrei Aleksandrovich is retired now, and dreams of visiting his island home, although it has been inaccessible for decades because of nuclear testing done there.

Andrei Aleksandrovich showed me the city of Arkhangelsk, the new and the old districts, the high-rise buildings, the blocks of old wooden houses now being painstakingly restored. I set out on a walk around the city with him on a Sunday. The sky was cloudy and snow fell lightly. It was only 14°F, not very cold. We walked the length of the embankment, where passenger ships stood ready for their winter stay. But navigation had not yet ceased. Ships loaded with lumber sailed by, overcoming the icy sludge; powerful tugs scurried about. Passenger navigation was over but the freight moved on.

I stand on the bank of the Severnaya Dvina as it freezes. Beyond are the White Sea and Arctic Ocean. The sun is already disappearing below the horizon; my faithful companion of many months' journey along the Soviet Union's icy reaches is already wintry, red, and tired.

S urrounded by ice hummocks, the Arkhangelsk travels the Murmansk-to-Dudinka line of the Northern Sea Route, bringing supplies to residents of coastal villages and islands of the Arctic Ocean. The entire navigation route follows the Soviet Union's northern coast, linking western ports with the Far East. The ship—namesake of a port of call since the 16th century—delivers its cargo and returns to Murmansk during "the season"—July to November. Later in the year, winter ice chokes off most seaports and icebreakers must clear passageways.

From the Chukchi Peninsula, springtime hunters launch their boat into the Bering Sea in pursuit of seals and walruses. At this season the animals lie on ice floes, sleeping sporadically as they guard against predators.

In open water, an Eskimo marksman takes aim as his Russian lookout keeps watch. Since the 1850s, rifles have supplemented harpoons.

Back on shore the hunter will butcher and share his ringed seal, or haul it home. A ringed seal is at peak weight in winter and early spring—some 200 pounds. Sealskin's durability makes it useful for boots and rough clothing.

247

The settlement of Khatanga sits on the tundra landscape just south of the Taymyr Peninsula, a mineral-rich area that stretches some 750 miles above the Arctic Circle. Khatanga is one of the world's northernmost coal producers. A fish-processing industry and river and air transport make Khatanga a hub for remote outposts. In their settlements and camps, the indigenous people also rely on hunting, fishing, and reindeer herding.

In winter on the Chukchi Peninsula, Eskimo workers from the Sereniki state farm rest easy, comforted by modern appliances and television shows beamed from Moscow.

249

W orkers from the sov-
khoz at Popigay cor-
ral reindeer in the
brisk November winds and
sub-zero temperatures of Taymyr. A traditional occupation
for Arctic peoples, reindeer
herding is now a productive
activity for the state as well.
Hardy, self-sufficient reindeer—the only domesticated
deer species—graze on tundra
lichens and herbs; the animals
require no planted crops or
winter shelter. Pound for
pound, reindeer meat costs less
to produce than beef. It gives
people a low-fat, high-protein
staple throughout the Arctic.

251

I nside a pen at a camp near the Popigay sov-khoz, a worker separates the animals. Some will be sent to winter pastures, where each reindeer requires at least 150 acres of forage. Others are slaughtered and the carcasses are hung to freeze and dry. Workers sort out the rest of the body parts. In addition to meat for a lucrative market, reindeer provide hides for floor coverings and pants, and suede hats, dresses, and slippers; fur stuffs mattresses and life preservers; leg skins become mukluks; antlers are for medicines and handicrafts; and tongues are pickled.

A farm worker skins a reindeer near the frozen Popigay River. Even in frigid weather carcasses may rot from the heat held in by their thick hides.

Nearby in Zhdanikha, Vladimir Ilyn cures reindeer skins for winter clothing and boots.

This Dolgan family—reindeer breeders of the Sopochnyy settlement—sometimes travels by snowmobile and sometimes by reindeer-drawn sled. Their settlement has wooden houses, a school, and a village hall.

Pages 256-257: Aboard his snowmobile, hunter-fisherman Valeri Ryabkov, a Russian resident of Taymyr, scouts for arctic fox and wild reindeer.

255

An armada of 40-ton *uragans* transports materials for constructing gas pipelines. Western Siberia's reserves, the largest in the USSR, produce at least 60 percent of the country's gas; over 118,000 miles of pipeline help distribute it.

Sparks from pipe welding light up the January darkness near Nadym, a tundra boomtown built in the early 1970s. Despite environmental protection laws, development of the gas fields around Nadym has destroyed millions of acres of grazing land, hurting reindeer and their Nenets herders.

259

260

A rtificial red caviar made at the Murmansk Fish Combine allows Soviet citizens to indulge a popular taste. The ersatz eggs, made of gelatin and casein, a milk protein, first appeared on grocery shelves in 1976, following ten years of research. As industrialization has encroached on spawning grounds, real caviar has become a delicacy rarer and higher priced than ever.

Traditional ice fishing prevails on the Bolshaya Polovinnaya River, in the Taymyr tundra, where Valeri Ryabkov's whitefish, a source of golden caviar, freeze almost instantly in the polar night.

The eternal flame honoring World War II defenders of the Soviet Arctic burns in Murmansk, a seaport 175 miles inside the Arctic Circle. Murmansk, said to be named from the Saami word meaning "the edge of the land," is one of the world's largest Arctic cities. Warm Gulf Stream waters keep its harbor ice-free, making it the nation's only port with year-round access to Atlantic sea routes. Established as a supply port in 1915, Murmansk received vital Allied aid for the embattled Soviet Union during World War II. Today its thriving fisheries and related industries employ much of the city's labor force.

Student teacher Irina Katukha celebrates the Festival of the Peoples of the North, an annual Murmansk event commemorating the end of long months of winter darkness. For more than 50 years the festival has been held at the end of March, although warm weather often doesn't arrive until July. The festival's 36-mile cross-country ski marathon attracts thousands of Russians and foreigners. More traditional events too are held. In a lively contest, reindeer herders race their animals in teams of four that pull wooden sledges.

Members of the Mur- *mansk Winter Swim- ming Club—known as Walruses—jog along a frozen path. Walruses claim that ex- ercising in the winter air un- locks the secrets of good health. While she trains to swim the Bering Strait, teacher Anna Litvishko—outfitted in a red swimsuit—runs about five* miles daily; she and her fellow Walruses finish their workout with a snowy rubdown.

During the March festival, spectators keep warm while club members take a plunge. Some Walruses say that noth- ing—not even changing poli- tics in Moscow—matters as much as keeping a swimming hole ice-free all year long.

Murmansk at night offers movies and plays at the white-columned Palace of Culture and Technology. By day students work at the Lenin Komsomol Murmansk Higher Nautical Engineering School, where they use computers for automatic navigation systems. The city's strategic location on the Kola Peninsula, base of the Soviet Northern Fleet, puts it in the midst of one of the world's largest military complexes.

With a wink and a wave, a naval engineering student gets ready to go on furlough with his comrades. In the future, when they sail the seas, they'll start from their vantage point at the top of the world.

Acknowledgments

We thank the persons and organizations named or quoted in *The Soviet Union Today*.

In addition we are grateful to the following for their generous help in the preparation of this book: George Demko, Dartmouth College; Basil Dmytryshyn, Green Valley, Arizona; Murray Feshbach, Georgetown University; Victor Mote, University of Houston; Andrea E. S. Lutov and Pritt Vesilind, National Geographic Society; Konstantin Likutov, Sergei Nikitenko, Boris Polkhovsky, and Nikolai Romanov, Novosti Press Agency; Metropolitan Pitirim, Moscow; Peeter Põlluveer, Tallinn; Roger Powers, University of Alaska; Felix Rosenthal, Moscow; Matthew J. Sagers, Bureau of the Census; Lee R. Schwartz, The American University; Shelley Sperry; Kathleen Trivers.

We received valuable assistance from the National Geographic Society Library and News Collection; Illustrations Library; Records Library; Administrative Services; Translations Division; Photographic Division; Production Services, Pre-Press Division; and Travel Office.

Index

271

Type composition by the Typographic section of National Geographic Production Services, Pre-Press Division. Color separations by Chanticleer Co., Inc., New York, N.Y.; The Lanman Companies, Washington, D. C.; Phototype Color Graphics, Pennsauken, N.J. Printed and bound by R.R. Donnelley & Sons Co., Chicago, Ill. Paper by Repap Sales Corp., New York, N.Y. Dust Jacket printed by Miken Systems Inc., Cheektowaga, N.Y.

Library of Congress CIP Data

The Soviet Union today / [prepared by National Geographic Book Service].
 p.   cm.
 ISBN 0-87044-816-1 (alk. paper).
 — ISBN 0-87044-817-X (deluxe: alk. paper)
 1. Soviet Union—Description and travel—1970- 2. Soviet Union—Description and Travel—1970- —Views.   I. National Geographic Book Service.   II. National Geographic Society (U. S.)
DK29.S48   1990   89-77839
914.7—dc20   CIP